PREFACE

When I wrote the book *Discus As A Hobby*, it was intended simply to share the information I had, thereby, perhaps encouraging others to take up the keeping of the most beautiful of freshwater fishes, the discus, genus *Symphysodon*. The success of this little book was greater than anything I expected at the time of its first release for publication.

I have received thousands of favorable reports and comments from discus hobbyists around the world.

It was because of this acceptance, as well as a review of all the current and past books on discus, that it became apparent that a detailed, follow-up book was justified. This work is intended to carry the hobbyist into the more advanced stages of discus keeping, in what I hope is the same easy-to-read, understandable format as *Discus As A Hobby*.

It is my intent in this volume to add to the information presented in that book and others and to do so in my own style. While I make no claim to total knowledge of the subject matter, I do feel that a less formal style of presentation will be gratefully received by the average reader. To those who are more interested in literary style than content, I can only suggest that they read other authors.

ACKNOWLEDGEMENTS

I would like to acknowledge the encouragement provided to me through both example and personal advice. The following individuals have often provided their direct knowledge and have been a great source of inspiration.

My wonderful and loving wife, Jane, while not sharing my interest in discus fish, has always encouraged my efforts to develop a large fish room. She has also lifted my failing spirits whenever my writing efforts have become difficult.

Dick Au is one real expert I have always consulted whenever I have had questions. His extensive insights have been invaluable. I consider Dick Au to be both unusually knowledgeable about discus fish and, more importantly, a friend.

Bing Seto is always full of boundless energy and is one of the few people I have met who is just a naturally talented discus keeper. Bing, thanks again for being part of the discus scene.

Another friend, Artie Davis, has extended his help whenever needed. When I met Artie Davis it did not take long to realize I had found a lifelong friend and soul brother. Artie has a generous nature and is one of the most kindly human beings I have ever met. In addition, he happens to be one fine discus breeder.

Last but certainly not least, I would like to thank Jack and Chris Moon, whose friendship I consider as beautiful as the discus I have treasured over many years. There are many others who should be acknowledged, but space only allows a limited few. But to all the others who must remain unacknowledged here, fear not, I know who you are and you are acknowledged in my heart.

DEDICATION

I dedicate this book to PFC James Henery Ramsey, who was killed in action on the Pacific island of Guam on July 21, 1944, and to all those who, like J.H., gave their lives so that others could live in a free society. Thanks to them, we can enjoy the pursuits such as those described in this book. Their sacrifices were the greatest gift one human can give to another, and will never be equaled or forgotten by a grateful, free nation.

Semper Fi.

"They made it for us."

TABLE OF CONTENTS

CHAPTER ONE

SUCCESS WITH DISCUS

I have been a keeper of discus for over 45 years. The enjoyment of spawning these and many other cichlids has filled thousands of hours with both learning and joy. It is time for me to pass along a little of what I've learned. Most of the information presented here was found the hard way: from trial and error, error, error. The systems and methods you find in this book have been used by me for quite a few years. While they may not be "the best way," they do work and work well.

Before we get into the meat of the matter, let me state clearly the goals of this book. The information stated here has been designed to help those who are more than casual keepers of the *Symphysodon* genus and those who would become more successful operators of small to large discus hatcheries. The information is geared to the more advanced hobbyist, but can be used by even the beginner to increase awareness of the procedures required to spawn and produce a high quality volume of discus fish.

It is recommended that at least 500 square feet be allowed for operating a small hatchery. Of course if more space is available, then the reader has an added advantage.

In this guide I will show you how to care for and produce thousands of quality discus per month in such a hatchery. Developing a market for such production, of course, is a different project. Some hints are included in this text.

While it is true that there are many different approaches to most of the requirements for keeping and spawning discus fish, it is also very true that not everything that has been written in current books is true or workable. Weeding out what is workable is very important to the small business person working a hatchery.

It is the aim here to start that process and to show in clear, easy to remember steps how to do that which leads to success on a repeatable basis.

Remember: Anyone can get lucky once in a while and get a successful spawn, but only those who are able to repeat the process time after time on demand are really experts or professionals.

" The information stated here...is geared to the more advanced hobbyist, but can be used by even the beginner... ."

SOME OF THE FEATURES
WE WILL COVER

Out of the information provided you will develop a day-to-day method that will ensure repeated success not only in spawning your fish, but also in developing better and better fish. You will also avoid costly failures.

In today's tropical fish market, anyone wanting to enter the hatchery business must compete with fish produced in large outdoor ponds in Florida, as well as pond-raised fish from Asia. Where does the small hatchery fit in? You must be able to fill a need not currently being satisfactorily addressed by the larger fish farms. This limits the selection of species the home hatchery can provide at a profit.

Based upon years in the business, only two species have provided such an opening for the small breeder: discus and angelfish.

Your success or failure will depend upon several things. First, being able to produce quality fish upon demand at reasonable prices. Second, remaining competitive by developing new strains or breeding new color types as they become hot in the market place. It is most important that you produce only high quality fish. The word will soon get around if you are turning out junk! In order to meet these conditions, you need a dependable method that is repeatable at will. At this point, a third factor comes into play: the time span from egg to market size fish. The faster you can grow fry to market size, the more profit you will realize per gallon of tank space and time spent. We will talk more about that later.

The overriding factor is Method, Method, Method. Once you are sure of your fish-producing method, you're on your way to success. Method is everything. Of course, understanding the biological functions of fish is important, too. For now we will only cover those aspects that affect health and spawning. There are many books on fish physiology. I strongly suggest *Aquariology* by Dr. John B. Gratzek, published by Tetra Press.

photo by Bing Seto

New red alenquer discus

THE FISH THAT STARTED IT ALL!

While it is not the aim of this book to offer detailed information about the wild species and possible sub-species of discus, it is still important to know at least a little about the wild types in order to form a basic idea about how we might improve them. So a very brief discussion of the wild discus is in order before we expand on the main points in the text.

The *brown discus Symphysodon aequifasciatus axelrodi* is most commonly referred to as the Wild Brown Discus." This discus lives near the mouth of the Amazon near Belem and up river in the slow-moving waters of the Rio Urubu, which feeds the mighty Amazon.

Discus are never found in the main or fast-moving waters of major rivers. The habitat provides an average pH of 5.4 to 5.8 and a softness of around 20 to 30 m/s. The fish are almost always found around fallen trees along the banks of slow moving streams.

This species was discovered by Dr. H.R. Axelrod. The coloration of the brown discus can be outstanding. Its rich, reddish-brown color, along with its bright red eyes, is stunning. The anal and dorsal fins are also brightly colored with red and orange and have black and blue streaking. With proper aquarium arrangements, they produce an outstanding display of discus beauty. The Brown Discus is perhaps the easiest of all the wild discus to care for and spawn. They become tank tame very quickly. For a long time now the Brown Discus has been ignored in the hobby. But recently the Asian breeders, who seem to be at the forefront of new color type development, have started using the wild brown in new crosses. In the near future you can expect to see the development of a 100% pure red discus from crosses with wild browns or perhaps the Wild Red Alenquer Discus or both.

Wild brown discus

The *blue discus Symphysodon aequifasciata haraldi*, is known as the Blue Discus. It is found in the wild near Leticia, Peru, the Purus river and in Manacapuru, Brazil. It is often referred to and sold as the Royal Blue Discus and more recently as Afanacapuru Blues. No matter what the common name, they are the same fish. The only difference is the intensity of the blue coloration. Again, this species or color type adapts well to captivity and will spawn with proper care and conditioning. The blue coloration is confined mostly to the dorsal and head regions. This fish has been used in crossbreeding for years; its bloodlines appear in almost all the discus produced for the hobby.

In fact, today's conglomerate of genetic codes found in such fish makes scientific development impossible. No one knows exactly what color types were used in the past to produce what you see today. It is like trying to put a jigsaw puzzle together without any markings or pictures printed on the pieces. In other words, your guess is as good as anyone's. But the rush to develop new color types without background information will go on. You just can't stop the mad hatter!

The *green discus Symphysodon aequifasciata aequifasciata*, has distribution in the Tefe River system and Lake Tefe, Santarem, and the Peruvian Amazon region. The coloration of the Green Discus shows a lot of yellowish-brown varying to light brown. The most notable marking of the Green Discus is, like the Blue Discus, around the head and gill areas. The notable feature is a more metallic sheen than that found in other wild species. While the vast majority of all wild discus are nearly round in shape, the Green Discus has a more oblong body shape. Perfectly round green discus are hard to find. The Green Discus has been used in the production of most color types found for sale, but in my estimation the proper mixing of the greens has been one of the missing elements that could produce outstanding, solid-body green fish.

I doubt that the Green Discus was used quite as much as the Blue Discus in the crossbreeding that produced today's array of discus selections. If anyone should be looking for a mostly unexplored breeding program, I would suggest using the green discus. The hobby market is just waiting for a good, solid-body green discus. If you were to develop one, fame and wealth could be yours.

We have cobalts and blues, which are super rich in color of selected types, but no green discus to match their beauty.

The *discus Symphysodon heckel* inhabits a geographical area in the Rio Negro, Rio Madeira, and the Rio Tombetas regions. This is the fish that started the craze that has lasted since it was discovered by Dr. Heckel in 1840.

photo by Jim E. Quarles

Heckel discus

A hundred and fifty-six years have passed since then and success in keeping and spawning Dr. Heckel's discus is still the accomplishment of only a few experts. Even with all our hard-gained experience , the Heckel stands alone as the goal of many expert breeders. This species of discus has special requirements not common to the other discus imported as wild fish. It demands super pure, soft water and temperatures much higher than those used in keeping the other species. This fish will sicken and die quickly when its demands are not met. All discus are demanding in their requirements for good health, but with the Heckel there is little room for error. You should never try to keep this fish in captivity unless you are willing to spend the time and funds required to supply its very demanding needs.

The *blue headed discus Symphysodon discus willischwartzi*, sometimes referred to as just the *willischwartzi discus*. I consider this a subspecies, but it is listed as a separate species at this time. It is one of the more desirable discus but is rarely found in the trade.

This species is characterized by its intensely blue head and gill areas. It also produces a lot of yellow color in the caudal, anal and dorsal fins. It is generally found in three regions of the Amazon: Lake Manacapuru, Rio Purus, and the Rio Tefe.

The fish named above are the species classified at this time, but that may change; a reclassification is underway that covers the entire cichlid group. Also, new color types are being caught and exported. I must say that from the standpoint of the average breeder it makes little difference how the discus winds up being classified. The main point to remember is that all species of discus crossbreed! All the artificial varieties are a combination and recombination of the wild fish listed here and perhaps others unknown to this writer. Until we go back and start over with wild species, no one will ever be able to sort out which combination produced which colors. This requires scientific methods and detailed record keeping, which have been lacking until now.

One of the greatest needs we have today is for some basic information about the genetic code of discus. While such studies have been carried out to some extent with angelfish, no one that I am aware of has engaged in mapping the genetic fingerprints of discus. To give you just a slight idea of the genetic makeup of today's artificial color types, suppose we

Red Scribbled Discus

design a wheel and on this wheel we mark 2000 numbers. Now place a nail at each number. To play the game you get to pick 50 numbers with the first spin of the wheel. But in order to win our game the numbers you selected must come up one after another without fail for all fifty spins of the wheel. Do you think you can do that? If you think that would be a hard game to play, trying to figure out the genetic make up of all the color types out on the market today would be twice as hard. Then, to add insult to injury, every Tom, Dick and Harry who is breeding discus comes up with their own descriptive names for their fish. Without belaboring the point, just remember that it is not possible under these conditions to consider any discus a true strain, other than one caught in the wild.

You will find the word strain misused a lot in books about discus, so don't be fooled. It is much safer and a lot more scientific to speak of color types rather than strains.

When breeding current color types, what is happening is what I refer to as the "if it looks good, spawn it" system. But beware. Many breeders work on a slightly different system: "if it swims and will breed, spawn it!" With all the negatives considered, we can still use the genetic types offered for sale. But remain aware of your limitations. Pick a color and type that has market value and start your breeding program. There is no reason why with a little common sense and a tad of scientific knowledge you cannot start producing a better discus starting with current stock. But keep records and develop a breeding plan. Don't just put a pair of fish together and let them spawn. Work toward a better discus at all times. We have enough junk out there on the scene now. Your byword should always be CULL, CULL, CULL.

We now come to the point for which you bought this book: discus and how to succeed in breeding them.

CHAPTER TWO

WATER, WATER, WATER

You will get sick of hearing the term water before we are done with this book. It will become your overriding concern when you expand into successful discus keeping. For without clean, soft, pure, slightly acidic water, you will always fail in keeping and spawning discus. Before going into the requirements of discus water, let's be perfectly clear about a few things.

Question: What is the difference between alkaline and total alkalinity? Most books on discus are not very clear on the subject.

Alkaline and total alkalinity do not have the same meaning at all. These are two different chemical terms that describe two different properties of water. They may appear to be very similar, but it is incorrect to use them in the same context. The term alkaline is correctly used when you describe a solution that has a high pH, that is a pH greater than 7.0. The measurement for alkalinity capacity, on the other hand, provides information concerning the stability of the pH; it is not a pH measurement.

On the other hand, water softness has nothing whatsoever to do with pH or total alkalinity, in a direct way. The properties of softness refer to the total dissolved elements or compounds in the water. When we speak of water hardness, we refer to a measure of the dissolved calcium and magnesium ions in the water, and of minerals such as calcite (calcium.) Most hobbyists never really grasp or fully understand the above principles when working with soft-water fishes.

You need not be a chemist, but you need enough understanding of water chemistry to be able to meet the basic needs of discus. The next major factor is the cleanliness of the water.

So how clean is clean? How pure is pure? How soft is soft? What is slightly acidic? Let's take the questions one at a time, okay? My idea of clean is water that is free of any substance that could be remotely harmful to discus. It should be free of most chemical substances or compounds. Would it be possible to use pure distilled water to keep and spawn discus? The answer is no! Not only discus, but all other fish as well, would suffer and die in such pure water. So how pure need the water be? The best we can do is make sure the water is free of known harmful substances, such as heavy metals, pesticides, etc. But

R.O. Water Unit

R.O. Unit with storage unit.

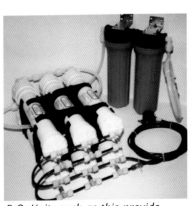

R.O. Units such as this provide ideal water for discus.

photos by Discus Haven Ultra Pure Water Systems, 539 Diana Ave., Morgan Hill, CA 95037

the water must contain the required trace elements the fish need to live.

We ensure this by adding back the trace elements after properly treating the water to remove other factors. In most places the tap water is not suitable for discus without first being treated with either an R.O. unit (reverse osmosis) or a twin filter arrangement. In the twin system, water passes through a cation exchanger. Whatever method is used, the resulting water will need to be adjusted using tap water, since the water from either system will equal almost distilled water without the proper trace elements. Discus seem to do best in water where the pH is between 5.8 and 6.8. However, in the spawning tanks the pH should be kept between 5.8 and 6.0 since this tends to help prevent egg fungus, as well as other bacterial problems.

Without clean, pure, soft, slightly acidic water you will always fail in keeping and spawning discus.

You should think of your water conditions as a set of ranges. Example: From 1 to 4, your water is ideal. The fish are healthy and eat and spawn well. The eggs hatch okay and the fry go to the sides of the adults to feed when ready, with no problem with lost or wandering fry. From 4 to 6, conditions are still acceptable, with fair results in the health and breeding. From 6 to 8, breeding starts to become a problem. A large percentage of the eggs will fail to hatch. The pair does not spawn as often as before, and the success in getting the fry to nickel size becomes much harder. From 8 to 10, breeding stops or the eggs fail to hatch. You will also notice that health becomes a problem, eating slows or perhaps stops, and stress becomes a problem.

It should be noted here that hard water in and of itself will not prevent keeping discus in reasonably good health. But breeding will become difficult if not impossible.

Breeding and successful hatching of the eggs is almost always dependent upon proper soft-water conditions. Once the fry reach the size of about a nickel you should change their water conditions slowly. They grow better in slightly harder water. I have always preferred to use grow-out water with a pH of 7.0 to 7.5 and a general hardness of about 250 to 300 m/s. This also provides a safety net when you sell or ship the fish, since the water they will most likely go into is generally less than ideal.

You have to get the fry to nickel size before worrying too much about new water conditions. Once you reach that point, developing the grow-out phase is easier.

One factor must be strongly pointed out here. Any and all changes of pH and temperature must be done slowly. Rapid changes will cause undue stress or even kill the fish.

PEAT MOSS:
THE DISCUS
BREEDER'S BEST FRIEND

Open any book written about keeping or breeding discus and you will find the subject of peat moss listed somewhere in the text. Generally, however its use is only casually covered. Over many years I have found that peat moss is without a doubt the most dependable and safest medium for conditioning your water once the basic requirements have been met.

This substance is fairly cheap and easy to find in almost any location. I recommend only Canadian White Peat Moss. Make sure it is pure with no additives.

Pick the lowest pH rating you can find. For a small operation, a filter frequently charged with peat will work fine. For the larger operation where large volumes of water are to be filtered, a larger arrangement is required. I use a 55- gallon plastic drum with a power head installed to keep the peat moss churning within the drum until water is pumped into the discus system. It requires that I recharge or replace about one cubic foot of peat moss once each month. Frequency of changes depends entirely upon the volume of water exchanged in normal operations.

The advantages of using peat are that
(1) it softens the water slowly and
(2) it adds back trace elements as it is doing so. Another advantage is that changes take place over a longer period of time, providing better control over pH changes. Of course, the use of peat will cause your water to turn slightly tea-colored.

Photo by Bing Seto. Discus World, Alameda, CA

Red turquoise discus tending their eggs

For a commercial enterprise this is no problem, but in a display tank you might want to filter the water through carbon to remove some of the tea color, yet retain the softness provided by the peat moss.

The proper mixture of tap and treated water will vary depending upon the local water supply. Generally, those depending upon well water or ground water will face greater problems than those whose source of water is provided by what is commonly referred to as surface or lake water. But no matter what the source of your water may be, peat moss will aide you in maintaining good discus water.

What needs to be stressed is that the above water conditions are not options, but basic requirements. Problematical water will never allow you to succeed. So, as stated, think and live Water, Water, Water.

As a mater of common sense, massive water changes will make it difficult to maintain the pH at any constant level. But the advantages of massive and frequent water changes will prove to be of more help than most realize. If the pH does not go above 7.0 and the softness can be retained at 30 to 50 m/s, you need not be too concerned about the slightly higher pH. You will find that the softness is far more a controlling factor in breeding than pH. If you feel you need to adjust the pH as part of your water changes, you should do so in your holding tanks and check to make sure you add new water slowly when replacing dumped water. Sulfuric acid works best with this method. Don't waste your money on weakened, store-bought solutions. Most simply contain water and sulfuric acid anyway. About 1 drop per 25 gallons works fairly well in maintaining a pH of 5.8.

How clean is clean? When making your water changes, wipe down the inside surfaces of the tank. Discus give off a slime from their bodies and this forms a film on the inside of the tank. This then becomes a breeding ground for bacteria. You want your bacteria in the filters, not on the glass. Before we move out of water conditions and on to other aspects of the subject, I will pass along my standard for clean tank water; if you are not willing to drink out of the tank then don't expect discus to remain healthy in it. The other control parameter is temperature. Keep your tanks between 82° and 86° at all times. Anything below 82° is not safe or healthy for discus.

WATER MOVEMENT
OR WATER CURRENTS

In a lot of ways discus are strange fish. One of the things they don't like is a lot of current in the water. They tend to be what I refer to as lazy fish.

They kind of like to move slow and easy and sort of peck at their food on the bottom of the tank. Fast water currents in discus tanks should be avoided if at all possible. While power filters are recommended, the return water flow should be baffled as much as possible. This is very important in spawning tanks. Discus males are weak spawners, so you should make every effort not to wash away the sperm before it can fertilize the eggs.

Once you have a successful spawning pair, try to maintain the same conditions at all times. One of the things I stress is, "if it isn't broken don't try to fix it." Don't make any radical changes to your water or its movement once you have a working method. One of the things I see breeders do is move spawning pairs of discus from tank to tank! Wrong! Once you have them happily married, don't disrupt their happy home life.

I try never to move a pair unless it becomes absolutely necessary for some unavoidable reason. One of the biggest problems people have in trying to breed discus is that they do things in a haphazard fashion. This, in large part, comes from moving fish around from tank to tank and not developing consistent methods in the fish room.

We will have to return to the subject of water later on. But some basic concepts must be understood and then you will see why certain aspects need repeating until the principles involved become second nature to you.

photo by Bing Seto

Second generation Brilliant Blue

TANKS: THEIR PROPER PLACEMENT AND CARE

If you are setting up a tank just to enjoy the beauty of the discus, you are not confronted with the same requirements found in the breeding hatchery. But if you are trying to spawn discus on a larger scale, then you must meet an entirely different set of conditions. For spawning pairs I recommend 20-gallon to 30- gallon standard size tanks, not show tanks. Show tanks are too narrow for discus spawning purposes. The tank need not be higher than 18 inches and should not be wider than 24 inches.

The physical placement of the tanks is of prime importance. Discus are shy, easily frightened fish. Physical movement in front of or near the spawning tanks should be avoided as much as possible. For this reason, most professional and advanced discus keepers have learned to place the spawning tanks up high. It has been found that if you arrange your spawning tanks so that the bottom of the tank sits at eye level, the stress to the fish is greatly reduced. Dim but serviceable light is also important, but we'll cover lighting suggestions later in the text.

Of course the total number of tanks you will need depends upon the intended size and desired output of the hatchery. Tanks are generally arranged in banks to meet these needs.

The grow-out tanks need not be placed up high, but should be maintained at about 32 inches from the floor. Tanks placed below 32 inches would most likely require special heating to offset the lower temperatures near the floor. I have found over the years that every breeder just kind of winds up with an oddball assortment of tanks.

Photo by Bing Seto

Brilliant blue and red turqouise crossed pair

But some planning needs to be done when laying out the fish room. First, of course, are the development tanks. This is where you will grow the fish you select as breeders to start the operation. The larger these are, the better. I prefer tanks of 135 to 150 gallons for this purpose. The fish grow faster, and the water quality is less critical over a given time span. I use two 135-gallon tanks for growing out breeders to an age of about 11 to 12 months before selecting them into pairs. If you can afford it and have room the more large tanks you have the better. In any event, you will also need a few 1- to 2-gallon tanks to hatch out eggs you intend to raise artificially. The you will need some 10- gallon tanks to grow very young fry to about the size of a penny before moving them into larger grow-out arrangements. I recommend an assortment of tanks, from 1 and 2 gallon through 10 and 20 gallon, all the way to the larger tanks needed. The wider the assortment the better.

The physical placement of the tanks is of prime importance. Discus by nature are shy, easily frightened fish.

One other consideration is heating the tanks to the proper temperature. Individual heaters can really add to your expense. I suggest room heaters with fans to properly move the air around the room. When setting up your tanks, take into consideration the air supply you will need to install them. Most hatcheries use turbo blowers and pipe the air through in 2-inch pvc pipe. So allow for this construction when laying out your plans. You will need a high volume air supply with medium to low air pressure. Using an individual air supply for each tank is not practical in most hatcheries.

OXYGEN, OZONE AND
GENERAL AIR REQUIREMENTS

Most people have heard the term ozone, and maybe even in connection with keeping fish, but little has been said about it with regard to discus. Almost no detailed information is given in the current crop of books about discus. Yet ozonization of aquarium water should be understood. You need to understand its good points as well as its bad effects.

Ozone generators are now offered more and more to the hobbyist, and they do indeed have a proper place in fish keeping. But great care must be taken when applying their use to discus tanks. The main purpose of ozone is to break down free waste and promote protein clotting.

In saltwater tanks, ozone aides in skimming unwanted protein from the water. In freshwater tanks, however, the effects of ozone are greatly reduced. It does perform a useful function, though, in oxygenating and enriching the water with a higher level of free oxygen. It also helps break down animal and fish wastes into a gaseous state, which is then partially removed by airflow within the water.

photo by Bing Seto, Discus World, Alameda, CA

Possible cross with alenquer red discus

The major drawback is that it also has a less than desirable effect on the mucus surfaces of the discus, which is the feeding layer on the spawning fish. Prolonged use of ozone in a discus tank should be avoided. I would recommend that you forego the use of an ozone generator in the discus hatchery. While ozone aides in removing or controling certain external parasites, the dangers in its use outweigh its advantages.

A much safer way to make your water parasite free is to use of ultraviolet light to sterilize the water. In the next chapter, the proper use of ultraviolet light will be detailed.

free is to use of ultraviolet light to sterilize the water. In the next chapter, the proper use of ultraviolet light will be detailed.

The last remaining remark about tanks and holding capacity is that whatever arrangement you decide upon, make sure you are not forced to overcrowd your fish. You must allow enough tank volume to handle the expected production of fry to adults to be used as breeders. Overcrowding produces stress and disease factors, which cannot be allowed.

photo by Bing Seto

Hatchery showing breeding tanks and piping for filters.

CHAPTER THREE

FILTERS AND RELATED EQUIPMENT

When designing the hatchery you must of course consider the type of filters you intend to use. This is especially important in the spawning tanks. In this chapter we will detail most of the filter types in current use and their best function in relationship to discus culture.

Since the object is to produce fry, you must be concerned with the safety of those very small fish from the instant they become free swimmers. Sponge rubber filters will meet this requirement quite nicely, and in addition they are easy to clean and care for over long periods of time. They only need to be rinsed out in clean, warm water from time to time. The pores are so small that the fry will not become trapped or be sucked inside them. Plus they offer another great advantage. When feeding fry small, live foods such as newly hatched brine shrimp, they become caught on the surface of the sponge; it then becomes a perfect feeding ground for the young fry. Since the fry are accustomed to feeding on the dark sides of the adults, they are naturally attracted to the dark sponge.

However, sponge filters must be of sufficient size so as to provide enough filtration for the fry. Don't forget the two, fully adult breeders sharing the tank with them.

The nitrogen cycle plays an important role in keeping your tank healthy. The proper filtering system promotes the nitrogen cycle.

THE NITROGEN CYCLE

Almost all filters work through a buildup of bacteria on the surface of the filter medium. There are several types of bacteria that change waste and chemical products in the tank into less harmful compounds.

With sponge filters and most other filters, these bacteria start building large colonies. The bacteria use harmful chemicals and compounds, such as ammonia, as food. Their own wastes change such chemicals into nitrites, which are further reduced to nitrates, an important element for chemical balance in the tank. This is known as the nitrogen cycle. The bacteria involved are called nitrosommus. It takes a good deal of time for the bacteria to establish themselves in sufficient numbers to make the tank safe for fish. The filter in question will go through different stages as the bacterial cultures build.

Ammonia is deadly to fish; so is too high a nitrite level. Nitrites prevent oxygen from being taken up via the gills. If you notice fish hanging near the top of the water, check the nitrite level of your water.

You will quickly learn just how import testing for ammonia and nitrites is as we go along with our study. If you are not sure just what is involved in the filter cycle, I suggest further reading on the subject.

One word of advice here may prove helpful and prevent costly mistakes. *If you ever feed live worms, do not allow them to come in contact with a sponge filter.* They will enter the filter, and eat it but they cannot digest the rubber. They will die in the filter. This becomes quite a mess and can quickly foul the tank.

While on the subject, I do not recommend feeding live or frozen tubifex worms to discus. But in spite of what I write or recommend, or what others have repeatedly stated about the dangers of this food, people will ignore the best advice and do it anyway.

Once you start feeding tubifex worms to discus you have started them on a road to a short life span filled with disease problems.

Now back to filters. Before moving on to other types of filters, let me point out that it is a good practice to use two, independent sponge filters in each tank. This way you can remove them one at a time for cleaning without upsetting or unbalancing the filtration of the tank. Never totally clean sponge filters unless you have suffered a disease problem in the tank. Never clean them with hot water or really cold water, and of course never use soap. Just wash them lightly in lukewarm water and use them again before they become dry. You want to retain as much of the nitrosommus as possible on the surface. If you kill off the bacteria while cleaning, they will have to go through the process of cycling again before they become effective again as filters.

POWER AND CANISTER FILTERS

When setting up a fish room, you always wind up with a wide assortment of different types of filters, some of which work better than others. Each have certain advantages and disadvantages that limit their use. Electrically powered filters have been around a long time. They come in all sizes and shapes. There must be a hundred or more companies that advertise and sell them. Then, there is the air operated flow filter, which has been around a lot longer. But other than using some form of power to move the water through the filter, they all work on the same basic principle. Each contains some form of medium on which bacteria grow and develop, plus they feed solids into the hold bed thereby helping to keep it out of the tank. This collection of waste presents one of the major drawbacks in using this type of filter. Rather than removing waste from the system, it only collects it in a confined space. Frequent cleaning is required. This involves more than just rinsing out the unit and starting it up again. Generally, the medium must be replaced and with it goes the beneficial bacteria culture you worked so hard to develop. The medium in these units can be a lot of different things: floss, rocks, carbon, peat moss or dozens of other items. Most of these filters are too small and need cleaning too often to be of much use as biological filters in a hatchery setup.

The canister filter works better in some ways than the other power units. This is because you can use it to charge the tank with peat moss or other longer term items as a medium.

I cannot resist saying what I think of some of the new do-dads being marketed by Marine brand filters. I refer to those with cute little bio wheels that spin around as the water is pumped over them in one way or another.

These are what I call "look good, feel good, do very little" features. In my personal estimation they are worthless as far as increasing biological action to any real extent. They make a great impression on the buyer. They rack up the cost of the product, but add very little worthwhile benefit to the systems in which they are used.

I must state that Marine Products does make a fine line of power filters; the Mag 350 and one called the Hot Shot are excellent filters. The Mag 250 is not near as good a performer as the others. These filters handle a very large volume of water over a given period of time and I have found them extremely useful in grow-out tanks. But come on folks! Knock off the cute stuff and just give us a good solid dependable filter! There are hundreds of brand names to pick from when buying this type of filter. Most perform about the same. Just compare cost and replacement parts when making your selection.

These red scribbled discus are the result of good water management and proper feeding. They are nearly breeding size.

When using these filters it is vital that frequent break down and cleaning be performed. Overall, canister filters will perform better long-term water treatment than the hang-on-the-side-of-the-tank type power filters.

CENTRALIZED
FILTRATION SYSTEMS

What is meant by the term central filtration? In this arrangement, all tanks in a given bank or selection of tanks are drained or pumped through a central filter system. The same water flows through all tanks from one centrally located filter. All the tanks need to be drilled for water discharge at a given level. This is fairly easy to do with brand new tanks and when building from scratch. Oil-soaked diamond bits allow you to drill through the tank wall at chosen locations. It gets to be tricky with old, used tanks; the glass becomes brittle and breaks more easily, so great care must be taken. The way this system works is quite simple: water is drained into a pre-filter via pvc piping and then allowed to flow into a filter bed with some sort of medium. This is generally a wet-dry arrangement arranged so that the water is sprayed over the medium or allowed to drip through it. The water then drops into a sump and is pumped back into the tanks via another set of pvc pipes with valves at each tank to control the return flow. Once again, the bacterial action takes time to build up on whatever medium is used. A pre-filter is used to catch all the solids that might enter the setup, and this is cleaned frequently.

photo supplied by Discus World, Alameda, California

Centralized filter system

In passing I should explain about using carbon in any type of filter arrangement. Discus hate carbon. It causes stress in the fish if exposure is constant. If you intend to use carbon in the system, use it to treat incoming freshwater only. Do not cycle filtered water through carbon back into the tanks. Once carbon is used, it quickly becomes a leaching agent for all the bad stuff back in the water.

I do not recommend the use of carbon in discus breeding. But if your water supply requires that kind of purification before use, then the best way to use it is in a pressurized tank hooked up to to your tap water supply. These tanks are provided by water treatment companies. They look much like standard pressurized oxygen units. They can be installed in minutes as needed. In most cases, they contain about 75 cubic feet of activated carbon.

Mr. Bing Seto of Discus World, Alameda, California, uses such an arrangement. It must work because no one can say Bing does not produce lots of absolutely beautiful discus. Just in passing let me tell you that Mr. Bing Seto has one of the most advanced hatcheries in the world. If you ever get a chance to tour this hatchery and meet Bing Seto, please do so.

RECENT ADVANCES
IN SAND FILTERS

Ocean Nutrition recently introduced the fluidized filter to the hobby market. These filters appear to offer fantastic advantages to of small hatcheries that elect to use central filter systems. Their use as individual tank filters, of course, would be limited by the cost of so many units being required.

This filter works slightly differently than most other types; water is pumped through a bed of fine sand particles. This causes the sand to become fluidized within the confines of its container. The surface area of even a small volume of such sand offers a huge area for bacterial cultures to develop. If you combine this with ultraviolet light the filtering effect becomes outstanding. The fluid bed filter requires the use of a powerhead type pump, and in some arrangements two pumps are utilized. For those designing a new system, this indeed seems like the way to go. With a proper pre-filter cleaning, recharging the fluid bed should not become a problem for a very long time.

Fluidized sand filter
Quick Sand, Bio-Con Labs,
Gainesville, Florida

WET AND DRY DRIP SYSTEMS

As saltwater fish keeping started to become more popular, there was a drastic increase in the development of the wet-dry filter system. In this arrangement, the water is generally allowed to free flow out of the tank into a pre-filter chamber filled with filter floss, then into a container that is filled with some sort of high surface area material, such as bio balls. There are hundreds of items on the market that can be used in drip chambers, all of course claiming to have the greatest surface area.

These filters work on the same principle as all the others. They allow the growth of bacteria on a large surface area. This type of filter does have one major disadvantage, though.

As the water is allowed to flow over the medium, it is supposed to just keep the surface area wet, thereby allowing bacterial growth to take place and become constant. The problem arises when channeling occurs. That is to say the water forms channels and some areas are left dry. When this happens, you lose part of the bacteria. Spray bars and drip plates prevent this, but not 100%. You always have some channeling.

This system works quite well in most hatcheries if properly designed and maintained. With the use of ultraviolet light in the water, return lines to the tank can be very useful.

Discus hate carbon. It causes stress in the fish if exposure is constant. If you intend to use carbon in the system, use it to treat incoming freshwater only.

In addition, it becomes easy to discharge a given percentage of water and arrange for the automatic return of the water to the central system. I do this with a simple overflow pipe. I allow about 20% of the old water to overflow into the drain, and this amount is then replaced via a float valve on the tap water supply.

Mr. Bing Seto has six central systems designed much like this and they work 24 hours per day. This is the system most likely to be found in operation in most medium to large discus and angelfish hatcheries in the United States. It works quite well and can handle a very large bio-load when operated with the proper water pump system. It is perhaps the cheapest method of filtering a very large volume of water on a dependable basis.

photo by Bing Seto

Red scribble female

THE DIATOMACEOUS EARTH FILTER

Diatomaceous earth (D.E.) is a powdery natural material that is formed almost entirely from the skeletons of diatoms, most of which were deposited in beds during the Cenozoic era. It is extremely fine in texture and gray or white in color. When in a pure state, diatomaceous earth is made up entirely of silicon dioxide or silica. Because it is so fine, it is often used as a filtering medium and has the ability to filter out even particles as small as bacteria.

This type of filter is very useful for polishing water in a show tank for public display. Since even the smallest particles are removed by this filter, the water has a crystal clear appearance. It really is a shame that this filter has so many disadvantages in relation to the normal small hatchery.

Let me explain briefly how this filter works and you will quickly note the problem areas. To charge or load the diatomaceous earth filter, it is necessary to install it in a closed system. Example: A five-gallon bucket would do. You fill the filter with water and start pumping, with the input and the output hose in the five-gallon bucket. Sometimes these pumps have to be primed before they will start pumping water. I do this by holding the entire unit upside down to start the prime. This causes what little air that remains in the system to be pumped out. Once you get the pump running, you then add about two or three cups of diatomaceous earth to the bucket.

The filter is built in such a way that a covering of porous canvas or other fiberous material prevents the D.E. from passing through it. Some of course will leak past and the larger particles will start to build up on the surface. Once this build-up has reached a certain point, it will trap even the smallest particles of D.E., and when the water starts to run clear and clean you are ready to transfer the intake and return hoses to the tank being filtered.

I have found these filters to be a real pain to work with. Most of the time when you transfer the hoses, part of the caking effect will break away and you always get some of the D.E. into the system.

These filters require very frequent cleaning and recharging with D.E. and therefore are not very useful in the commercial hatchery.

If you are handy with tools, I would suggest making a much larger unit than is presently on the market. All you really need is a fairly large volume pump and a container to hold the units covered with fabric that coat with D.E. powder. All this can be built with pvc piping and is easy to charge and clean with a set of intake and discharge valves, if designed right.

If you use this type of filter, it should only be used to polish the water after all solids have been removed by a pre-filter or other system.

The system should not be operated full-time in any discus arrangement. The filter is simply too good to be true. It will remove too much from the water if operated 100% of the time.

KEEP YOUR WATER CLEAN

• *FREQUENT WATER CHANGES*

• *SAND FILTERS*

• *WET/DRY DRIP SYSTEMS*

• *DIATOMACEOUS EARTH FILTERS*

photo by Bing Seto

Bing Seto tending tomorrow's breeders

THE UNDER-GRAVEL FILTER
BETTER KNOWN AS THE FILTH COLLECTOR THAT KILLS DISCUS

The best thing I can say about using one in a discus tank is don't even think about it unless you like sick and dead discus. In spite of all we have learned and all that has been written about safely keeping discus over the past 20 years, there are still people who spend a lot of money buying good discus and then send them on the road to ruin in tanks with under-gravel filters. The principle that clean water is healthy water is out the window when you confine filth under a layer of gravel with the foolish notion that out of sight is equal to out of the system and therefore safe.

If you were to wash out the gravel a couple of times per week, then perhaps you could manage to keep disease under control in such tanks. By washing out the gravel, I mean removing it from the tank for cleaning and replacement, not just kind of moving it around with a siphon hose hoping to remove the filth. Even then you would have a layer of filth under the plates used with these filters. As you can judge from my remarks, I do not think very highly of this type of fish filter arrangement. I think even less of people who have been warned and use them anyway. I know the argument that if you want a planted tank you have to have gravel, and that if you have gravel you should put under-gravel filters in to help keep things clean.

What a royal joke that argument is. If you have ever used such a filter for even a couple of months, then broken down the tank for cleaning, you will remember what a foul stench came from the tank. If you intend to use these filters, I suggest you just go ahead and feed the discus to the cat and be done with it. Don't waste your time and make the fish suffer. Regardless of what filter you use, remember that frequent, massive water changes are your best filter. Don't depend on any filter to replace water changes.

I know that there are those who will ignore what I have said about under-gravel filters and use them anyway. So here is a suggestion for those who want healthy plants in the discus tank. Confine your plants to those species that will do well in acidic water with subdued lighting. Then plant them in fired red clay pots. You can fill the bottom of the pots with planting soil and put a nice heavy layer of gravel or rock over the surface to keep the soil from floating out. This will allow you to move the potted plants around as you keep the bottom of the tank as clean as recommended. Just remember, if it's in the tank it needs to be kept clean. Wipe down the foliage from time to time to remove slime, just as you do to the insides of the tank. Clean, Clean, Clean.

CHAPTER FOUR

LIGHTING

IN THE HATCHERY OR BREEDING ROOM

Lighting plays a role in the production of discus in hatchery settings. In the average community tank, six to eight hours of standard white light seems to work well.

But in a breeding operation, the light requirements are quite different. I have found that normal lighting works during the day for work chores, but breeding discus requires 12 to 14 hours of fairly strong light per day. At night the light should be subdued but still strong enough for the fish to be able to move about and feed if they desire. Yet it should be dark enough that they tend to go into a total rest period. You should avoid total darkness.

The best reason to keep some subdued lighting on all the time is to prevent shock should the lights suddenly be turned on. I have seen discus dash themselves to death on the sides of the tank when bright lights were turned on out of total or near total darkness.

I recommend a dimmer switch be installed so that lighting can be increased slowly when needed.

I have not covered lighting requirements for plants for the simple reason that I see no need to keep plants with breeding discus. After all, that is what this text is all about: breeding and spawning discus.

At this point we should speak a little about the temperament of discus in general. I have collected and read most if not all the books in print, and quite a few out of print, that cover the subject of the pompadour fish. In very few has the subject of the basic temperament or psychological nature of discus been mentioned, much less been the subject of study.

The more you understand about their basic physical and psychological reactions, the better prepared you will be to meet their needs. It is not enough to know that discus eat, swim, and breath oxygen from the water, nor is it enough to just know how to keep the water clean and disease free. You need to understand the very nature of your fish.

Discus are very easily stressed; they are shy and retiring by nature. Don't get the idea that among themselves they are meek little lambs. When together as a group, they establish their own pecking order. One fish will always be king of the hill, followed by the next fish in line. Should the king fish be removed from the tank, the challenge starts all over again until a new boss takes over.

Even when bonded pairs start their courtship for spawning, love is not always gentle. Like most other cichlids, discus defend areas. Should three fish be together and bonding or mating should occur between two of them, the third will be driven away and perhaps even killed unless removed from the tank. The act of love or bonding can be a rough game. So keep yourself aware of bully males. They can and do become killers at times.

You may even find a male now and again who just hates all other discus. With a fish like this, give it a chance to become sociable, and if it still fights and harms other fish, it has been my experience that the best solution is either to give it away or kill it. A discus that will not spawn is a worthless mouth to feed in a hatchery or fish room.

You should also be aware that not all nice, healthy discus will spawn as adults. Some just never seem to be interested in procreation. These are hard to spot and it takes a lot of time to weed them out of your breeding stock. It is heart breaking when this happens after a year of tender, loving care and the male turns out to be the best-looking fish you have. But it happens, so be aware of the problem.

You need to learn to spend as much time as possible studying the individual fish in your discus collection. If you learn the ways of discus, you will find a great deal of difference between individual fish in any tank. But learning how they react and socialize as individuals will always increase both your knowledge and your chances of success when spawning them.

THE UNPLEASANT TASK

If you keep fish, sooner or later you will be forced to deal with fish that must be killed. This is a matter of simple common sense. A worthless discus is just that, worthless. It is not only non-productive, it is an added stress factor in the hatchery, both for you and perhaps the other fish. Weak or sick fish are a danger to other discus. No one likes the job of killing a fish or pet. But sometimes it must be done. The way I prefer is quick and sudden. I simply take the fish in the palm of my hand and quickly throw it to the concrete floor.

The sudden shock is instant death to the fish. No pain is felt, as far as can be observed.

Another way is to place the fish in a plastic bag with just enough water to float. Then place that in the freezer. As the water turns cold and freezes, the fish simply lowers its vital signs and dies. Again, it seems painless, but who knows for sure? Of course, for those who cannot bring themselves to do either chore, there is always the cat! Never give away a sick or deformed fish. Cure it or kill it. Passing along disease to another fish keeper is not a very friendly thing to do.

Aside from diseased or sick fish, you will have to ruthlessly cull for deformed fish or fish that just do not come up to the very high standards you should set for yourself.

We discus breeders live in a very small world. There is not a day goes by that I do not hear horror stories about someone who sparked joy in someone's life by not maintaining super standards with regard to his fish or business. So be on guard. Maintain such a high standard that no one would dare question your stock.

CHAPTER FIVE

BUYING DISCUS

FOR STOCKING OR STARTUP

When you reach the point where you're ready to buy your start-up stock, you must invest wisely. Just what you decide upon as starter stock will set the stage for at least a year into your operation.

A WORD OF WARNING

There are hundreds of people selling discus in the United States. There are thousands selling discus in Asia. Not all are honest in either place. So you should investigate those from whom you plan to place orders for breeding stock. A little time checking the references of people with whom you plan to do business can and will save you time, lots of money, and a good deal of heartache later.

Ask for references. Get two or three and take the time to check them out! Check with the editors of the major hobbyist magazines and see what, if anything, they know about the individual in question. But be aware that you cannot rely upon what one breeder says about another breeder. A lot of breeders are fairly petty when it comes to competitors, so be aware of the art of bad-mouthing that goes on from time to time.

There are basically three ways you can start your program when buying your starter stock.

   1. You can buy fully adult, breeder size fish. This would be the fastest way to get into actual production. If you elect to do this, you can expect a great deal of expense but quick breeding results.

   2. You can select young adult discus that are 8 to 10 months old. These would be a good deal cheaper, but still would give you a good idea of what they will develop into as adults.

   3. You can decide to buy very young fish at the size of 2 1/2 to 3 inches. This is by far the least expensive way to get started. If you elect this option, you will need more information about the breeding stock from which they are derived because at this age and size not much can be told by looking at the fry. The color and finnage will not develop until the fish are at least 6 months of age. If you find fish that are small and very colorful, beware. They most likely have been colored with food additives or hormones.

Feeding color enhancers or hormones to discus is one of the most dishonest things a person can do as a breeder. Yet it happens all the time. So be aware of it when selecting your fish.

Of course there is a fourth way you can get started. You could shop around and buy mated spawning pairs. This is very expensive and there is some risk involved in doing so.

The pairs you buy might be spawning in their present setting, but may never spawn for you after they are shipped or moved. It's not likely but it happens sometimes. They could also be old, spawned-out pairs.

Starting with wild discus is the least expensive method, but be aware that the market for offspring of wild discus is very limited. You should consider it only to learn the trade and develop your breeding skills. The artificial tank hybrids are where the interest is right now. As to color lines or types, that is really a matter of personal choice.

The market is there for just about all the color hybrids currently available. Solid colored fish always sell well: the cobalts, the brilliant blues, and the old favorite the powder blue discus. Red striped fish are also in heavy demand. Mr. Bing Seto prefers the red type hybrids and has devoted most of his efforts along this color line. I think that Mr. Dick Au of South San Francisco prefers solid colored blue discus. In the last two or three years there has been a rush to buy the pigeon blood discus that arrived in the United States from Singapore. Mr. Jack Wattley has worked with these fish a good deal and crossed color types to develop a strain or color type he refers to as "Pandas." So as you can see, different strokes for different folks is the rule. The point being that it will be your choice. So check out the market and then select those that you feel will provide your sales base. Then you can add a few color types that you just want to work with yourself.

The tastes of discus keepers change quickly, but there is always going to be a market for the old standard reds and blues.

All you can do, as far as genetics is concerned, is note what you start with and try to develop a sensible breeding program to develop a better and more colorful discus. To further compound your problem of selection, no one has kept any real, long-term breeding records. So the route taken to any given color type is just a guess!

Since all discus can crossbreed and have done so in the past to produce the seemingly endless selection currently being sold, it stands to reason that a recombination and further crossing of current types back to wild stock could produce an infinite number of possible color types. When you consider the possible mutants, like the pigeon blood, being added to the gene pool, the possible color types are limitless.

Who knows what color type may be developed or appear in just a few short years? I am sure of one thing, the present trend of out crossing to produce different color types will expand in the years ahead. Always look for that lucky wild card that may appear suddenly in your grow-out tanks. It could be as good as a winning lottery ticket!

After all, Jack Wattley found one a year ago. So could you. Just keep looking and trying.

Where To Look
For Good Starter Stock

Look in the advertising sections of the hobby magazines Freshwater and Marine Aquarium Magazine and Tropical Fish Hobbyist Magazine. This should give you a good starting point. There are national and international discus clubs and societies you can contact or join. Get referrals from other people you know who keep discus or have done so in the past. As a last resort, E-mail or fax me for a referral list.

One thing you should demand if buying site unseen or via mail is that full color photographs of the breeders from which the fish are derived be sent to you before you buy. If a supplier cannot provide color photos of his breeding stock, I would back away from the deal quickly, even if the references check out in all other regards. Before going on, let me define some terms about discus breeders in general. If you accept the classification listed, I think it will clarify your understanding of the discus hobby.

Credit for this classification is given to Stan Lippmeir, Stan Skeba and Gerry Helmle.

An Advanced Hobbyist—Manages 3-10 tanks (100-500 gal). Spends 3-12 hours weekly on fish room operations. Occasionally sells small lots of discus to defray expenses. He remains a hobbyist.

A Professional Breeder— Manages 20-50 tanks (800-3000 gal). Spends 3-12 hours daily on fish-room operations. Sells discus frequently. Does little or no advertising. Does not regularly ship discus. He has a small business.

A Commercial Breeder—Manages all aquaria and equipment usually involving more than one person on a full time basis. Principle business is breeding, raising and/or brokering discus and discus related products for sale. Advertises in the various hobby and trade magazines. This is a commercial breeder and business.

Asian Discus
German Discus and
American Discus

Over the past few years, the spawning and breeding of discus has become big business in Asia. Japan is a very large marketplace for discus. But with Japan it seems to be a one-way street: a lot of discus are going in from around the world but very few are coming out or being exported. This is not the case with the rest of Asia. Singapore has become the center of discus export, followed by Hong Kong and Taiwan.

There are also import and export markets in and out of Germany. Some of the world's best discus breeders are located in Germany. I will not get into naming the names of world renowned breeders or hatcheries from these locations, but I will point out a few of my own observations about them.

I am sure there are some worthwhile fish that are bred and shipped out of Asia. It's just that I have seen about 98% pure junk sold from there. The wholesalers buy discus from Singapore based upon price and shipping costs, not quality. When you consider the diseases that are the result of feeding live sewage worms to discus in these hatcheries, you become gun shy about buying these imports. Also, the color additives and hormones that are used to color the fish for retail sales in the United States do not improve their standing much. I leave it to you to decide if you want to deal in this grade of fish. I personally do not!

I see lots of advertising and promotions in one hobby magazine for one well-known hatchery in Singapore along with lots of outstanding color photographs of their fish. But I have yet to see any fish of the quality shown being exported or received by anyone in the discus breeding scene here in the United States. Those that I have personally checked with found the experience anything but enjoyable or honest! In some cases, I guess if you are willing to spend the big advertising money you can get anything you want written up in the trades.

Now let's take a look at the German imports. I have personally received hundreds of young fish from German breeders. I have always found them to be excellent products.

I will name one well-known breeder whom I highly recommend. Dirk Schlingmann is one of the world's foremost breeders of discus fish. I have found his strains to be as close to perfect in body shape as possible. The colors are as advertised and vivid. Dirk always provides you with a descendent certificate, which states the blood lines of the strain sold. To the best of my knowledge, Mr. Schlingmann only sells fish he has produced and raised. He is not a broker of an unknown's fish.

Now that I have made a lot of people mad at me with the above remarks, it is time to make a few observations about American produced discus. In America we have a wide range of discus breeders, some excellent, some good, some fair, and many who are bad! How do you go about selecting those who produce good fish from those who do not? One word explains it! Reputation. Depend upon it. Check it out. It is a factor that is earned, not awarded.

BECOME PART
OF THE TRADE

Become a part of the discus trade. Join one or more discus interest groups or trade organizations. Read and write articles for publication. Learn and expand. Help others who are just starting out. Not everyone has the same abilities, but everyone can offer some input that will expand the trade.

CHAPTER SIX

FEEDING YOUR DISCUS

FEEDING ADULT FISH

The next important item we must cover is what to feed your fish. And just as important is how much and when to feed them.

Since we will cover this topic for both adults and fry, let's start with the adult fish. In the wild, discus feed on vegetable matter, insects, worms and other living organisms. In fact, their diet is quite varied and changes from season to season. When we are faced with proper feeding in the home or hatchery aquarium, we must keep in mind the varied diet aspect. It is true that you could feed them nothing but fake food and your fish would live and perhaps grow to full, adult discus. But they will always do better and remain healthier if you arrange to feed them some live food and vary the balance of the food between vegetables and some kind of high protein meat product. This can be earthworms, beefheart mix or perhaps, if you are really stupid, blackworms or tubifex worms. Frozen bloodworms are a great food source for the meaty part of their diet. The best way to think about feeding is to put yourself in the place of the fish. Suppose you were to pick even your most favorite food and eat nothing else for one full year. What kind of physical condition do you think you would be in at the end of your test period? I am sure you would be in very sorry condition. Aside from the fact that you would have lost all interest in your food, your health would be gone as well.

In the wild, discus feed upon vegetable matter, insects, worms and other living organisms.

Overall, I have found that using a beefheart mixture that contains some vegetables and high protein dry foods with a vitamin supplement keeps discus in good health and good breeding condition. You will find the formula that I use listed in the appendix of this book.

Discus will eat almost anything you give them if they are introduced to it the right way and if they are hungry enough. In most books you will find statements about what fussy eaters discus are! You should take such statements with a grain of salt, for they are just not true.

You will find recommendations about feeding them items such as glassworms, vinegar eels, waxworms, grubs, wingless fruit flies, etc. And yes, perhaps all these things are okay to feed them, but if you are like me, you will have enough to do around the fish room without the added problem of culturing bugs and worms.

If you have the time, and your wife will allow strange-looking creatures to

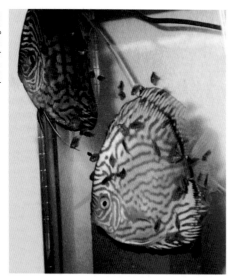

Red turquoise pair with fry

crawl or fly all over the house, then you can grow some of the items named above for your fish. The best food to grow is earthworms. Bite for bite, there is no better food for any type of fish. Discus thrive on them. Red earthworms are easy to culture. It can be done in plastic shoe boxes with a mixture of peat moss and planting soil, and they can be fed table scraps, a slice of bread, a little Gerber baby food, or dry, uncooked oatmeal. All you have to do is keep the mixture moist, not wet.

A lid is required with some kind of tight-fitting screen that will let in air yet not allow the worms to escape.

If you collect the worms while they are small, no processing is required, you just use them whole. If larger worms are used, a garlic chopper can be used to cut them into small chunks for feeding. Some people clean them before feeding them to their fish. This is done by placing them in a box for 24 hours with nothing but clean, chopped newspaper that is slightly damp.

Of course you can use them as I do, just chopped to small size. The process is a little messy but if you place the chopped worms in a fine net and run a little cold water through them, all that is left is worm meat. The fish could care less if they are cleaned.

Earthworms are a disease-free and parasite-free food that is safe to use at any time. I recommend that everyone use them as a principle source of food for discus.

FEEDING: FRY
TO ONE-INCH SIZE

Once you have a pair of producing fry, and even before the time arrives to remove them from the sides of the adults, you are faced with preparing the very small fry to eat on their own once they are moved away from the adults and start their grow-out phase. I recommend that when the fry are five to seven days old and still feeding from the parents, newly hatched brine shrimp be added to their diet.

You do this by using a cooking baster and just squirting a small amount of live brine into the group of fry gathered around the adults. If you're careful you can do this without alarming the fish. It is easy to tell when the fry start filling up on the new shrimp. Their little bellies will turn a kind of pink color. You should be careful not to overfeed them, because any uneaten shrimp will quickly foul the water . The adults also hate to have the little shrimp in the water. They swim into and around the gills of the adults and this bothers the fish a lot. It is harmless but it makes them jumpy and slightly stressed out. You should feed a dab of new shrimp to the fry for a least four days before moving them to their own tank. You have to make sure that all the fry are feeding on the shrimp before moving them otherwise some will die for lack of food. I use an eye dropper to feed the fry the newly hatched shrimp, that way I have better control over the exact amount fed.

It is tempting to sell substandard offspring to friends or to local pet stores. Don't do it.

On about the seventh day, start feeding them finely ground flake foods; this food needs to be ground as finely as fine pepper. Feed them very small amounts until you see the fry going to mid-water or feeding off the bottom of the tank. At the age of three weeks start feeding them finely ground beefheart mixture. Be very careful not to overfeed them. Remove any and all uneaten food from the tank about one hour after first feeding them. Any uneaten food will foul the water, but beefheart is really bad if left too long.

By the time you start feeding them beefheart, the fry should look like discus in shape and they should grow quickly from this point on. I recommend a 50% water change after feeding a tank full of fry from penny to nickel size.

Always feed them at least two hours before turning down the lights for the night.

As soon as possible after the fry are eating flake or dry food plus beefheart, quit feeding them brine shrimp. The sooner you can get them past their need for newly hatched brine shrimp the better. Brine shrimp are necessary for fry, but other foods, once the fry are able to eat them, offer a much better growth diet. With fry up to three inches, what you want is a high protein diet. The higher the better. Lean beefheart offers very high amounts of good protein. So basically what have we learned so far? Super Clean Water and Super High Protein Foods.

One other factor that is very important in tanks containing young discus is the need to wipe down the insides and bottom of the tanks every single day before water changes!

The slime buildup is fast and harbors bacteria blooms that can and will cause the onset of disease. Remember, baby discus require time to build defenses against disease. They are born helpless against an outbreak of parasites or disease producing bacteria.

I do not recommend that any bacterial agent be put into fry water. Should a problem occur, just add rock salt and make massive water changes. It is better to just dump a tank of sick fry than to try to treat them with antibiotics. In the chapter on fish medications you will find a list of products that can sometimes be used to great effect, but to my knowledge, no proven results about using any medication on discus have ever been published . So with experience as the best teacher, go easy with medications. Generally, I have found the use of antibiotics to be of little value in discus keeping.

photo provided by Jim E. Quarles, Discus Unlimited Hatchery, Orangevale, CA

Tender loving care provided by adult discus.
Experience is the best teacher.

CHAPTER SEVEN

PAIR BONDING OR MATING

EQUALS REDUCING STRESS

When I give lectures or talks to clubs, one of the major questions that always seems to come up is the bonding or mating of pairs. Everyone wants to know how to sex discus! Since I have been spawning discus for a very long time, people seem to think I should be able to just look at a tank full of them and pick male from female. I wish I could. I wish anyone could and could also explain their method to me.

The truth of the matter is that after you have worked with thousands of discus, you do seem to get the feel for being able to sex the fish. But I cannot really explain in words how I do so. It is just something you learn the feel for! But to tell the truth, I am only right about 80% of the time.

The best way is to let the discus pick their own mates. I will explain how I do this shortly. When I am really pressed to give an answer about how I tell male from female, I just tell people to watch the fish when they spawn. The one that lays the eggs is the female! But really, all joking aside, there are a couple of ways you can greatly increase your chance of success in mating a pair of fish.

photo by Bing Seto

Brilliant blue discus in the bonding tank

MATING OF PAIRS: METHODS USED

When you have fish that are between 11 and 14 months old, you should pick the group you desire to mate into pairs. Then place six to eight fish in a fifty-gallon, bare bottom tank with just a large sponge filter. In this tank place a spawning cone or red fire brick. I use one at each end of the tank and one in the middle. At this point I feed these fish very heavily with earthworms and a high protein dry food three to four times per day.

Good Food

Soft Lighting

A Little Dancing

Reduce the lighting somewhat and try to arrange the tank so that you can view what the fish are doing from some distance. The fish will mate quicker if there is little movement around the tank. It's not that the fish are bashful about their mating behavior, it's just that they do act differently in a stressed environment.

If the fish are ready to perform bonding, they will do a little dance, tail slapping with each other, perhaps even a little lip locking, pushing, and shoving. Two fish that are bonding for mating will rise toward the surface of the water, then bow their heads as they sink downward together. When the bond becomes stronger they will mark out an area around the spawning site they select and not allow any of the other fish to come near it. When you see this action or perhaps see them starting to mouth clean the sides of the bricks or the spawning site, it is time to move them to a spawning tank of their very own. As you remove pairs that bond, you can add new fish to the fifty-five gallon tank to replace them and increase your chances of more pairs forming.

Another way you can select pairs requires a little more effort on your part, but I have found it very useful and had great success with it.

In a twenty- or thirty-gallon, bare bottom tank, place three adult or near adult fish using a sponge filter for filtration. Place one spawning cone or red fire brick at one end of the tank and the sponge filter at the other end. Once again, you feed them extra rich, high protein foods. The fish that pair off will drive the third fish away from the area they pick as a spawning site. In fact, you must keep a close watch on these fish because the pair will damage the third fish and could even kill it if it is left with them for too long.

The fish will go through the same mating actions that were observed in the fifty-five gallon tank, only the bonding is generally done more quickly. So if you use this method, be aware of the danger to the odd man out.
If no bonding occurs, replace one or more of the three and try again. If the pair has bonded, they will drive the extra fish to the far end of the tank and

force it to stay near the top in a corner. Both of the fish that have paired off will attack the third fish from time to time.

Perhaps I should explain the term " bonding." I simply use the term to note that two fish have become compatible for mating at a given time and place. This is not a life-long bond. Discus pairs can be broken up and mated to other discus. So when I use the term "bonding", it simply means that two fish will spawn together, nothing more.

In the three-fish method, bonding will generally take place from within a few days to a week, sometimes even overnight.

Here I will tell you a little trick of the trade. If you want to speed up mating or increase spawning in a mated pair. After the fish have settled down in their new tank and the water conditions are stable at 82° to 84° F, drain about half the water (7 to 10 gallons.) Replace this with water from 60° to 65° F. In a lot of cases this will induce spawning within a few hours. A sudden change in heat will almost always induce spawning if the pair is in spawning condition. Also, a change in pH, within limits, will cause the same result. But rapid pH changes should be avoided at all costs.

If you try this and it does not result in success, wait a few days, feed the fish well with a rich diet and try again. I use this method when a pair goes off its regular spawning cycle once in a while.

One other factor plays a part in mating discus. Stress should always be kept as low as possible, but during bonding, reduce lighting and less movement around the tank will increase your success ratio.

Once a pair has formed, it is best not to move them around from tank to tank or place to place in the hatchery. They should be maintained in one tank for life, if possible.

If you move the fish you are likely to break the bond and this takes time to re-establish, and this, of course, cuts your fry production. Just one other aspect should be noted. Sometimes after spawning has taken place, one fish, be it male or female, will eat the eggs or fry. If this happens, remove the offending fish to another tank and let the remaining adult care for the eggs or fry. More about this will be covered a little later in the text. Sometimes the pair will start fighting over who is in charge of the eggs or fry and this makes for an unhappy home. One will most likely have to be removed until later when they can be rejoined for another spawning.

It has been my experience that the male generally takes better care of the fry than the female, but this is not always the case. Should you encounter an egg or fry eater, you will just have to watch and note which one of the pair is the guilty party. Sometimes both will do this until after they have spawned a half dozen times and learned that the fry and eggs are not food. But most pairs quickly learn to care for the eggs and fry without problems.

Sometimes when I have to transfer the male out of the spawning tank, I will use him with another ripe female until I can re-bond him to the first female. This works only if you have excellent male discus. Of course it does not work so well if you have to remove the female, since she requires longer to produce another batch of eggs.

In any case, once you have pairs that spawn, you learn which of the fish are male vs. female, and that gives you a great advantage.

CHAPTER EIGHT

THE ACTUAL SPAWNING

WHAT TO LOOK FOR

As you develop spawning pairs, you need to condition them with good, high quality foods and provide the proper lighting and water conditions. The pair will start cleaning a spawning site to lay their eggs. This may take anywhere from one hour to two or three days, depending upon the pair. Once they are satisfied with the site, the female will make several passes over the spot with her spawning tube extended. The first couple of times will generally be a dry run. But soon she will start depositing sticky eggs in a row on the cone or brick. Once she has put a few eggs down, she moves to one side and the male takes his turn gliding over the deposited eggs. He then moves away and they repeat the cycle until all the eggs are deposited. When the eggs are all in place, one or both fish will stand guard and fan the eggs with their fins, now and again using their mouths to clean something off the site. They do not move the eggs. Once deposited, they remain in the same place until they hatch out and become wigglers.

After about 72 hours the eggs start to hatch, at which time they remain attached to the spawning site by a thin sticky thread attached to the top of their heads. Should one come loose and sink away, the adult will pick it up and try to put it back on the site. As the fry age, they all come loose from the site; the adults give up trying to put them back.

Photo by Bing Seto

Once they become very active, the adults will sometimes move the fry from the spawning site to another location.

The next step for the young is a matter of life or death. While the fry are wigglers, they are living off the yolk sac of the egg. Once they become free swimming, they use up what little food is left and the sac disappears. At this stage they must swim to the sides of the adult to feed off the slime coat of the pair. Should they not do so for any reason, they will die within about 4 to 12 hours. If they do not locate the food source provided by the adults, they are goners unless you start feeding them artificially.

At night it is most important that they have enough light

Happy results!

to find and feed off the sides of the adults when needed. A dim light directly over the tank will work nicely for this purpose.

When you have very young fry feeding off the sides of the adults, I would stop the tank cleaning until they are five or six days old. At that time , they will hang like a cloud around the adults; careful cleaning can then take place. Be careful at this stage and do not overfeed the adults and foul the water. The young fish will die quickly in fouled water. Keep up your water changes but reduce the volume to about half the regular amount. Do not put live food in the tank for the adults at this time. If it moves, they will snap at it. Since young fry move, you do not want them used as food.

If the fry batch is very large, you should remove them at about 10 to 14 days of ages since they will damage the skin on the adults if left too long. You will just have to use your judgment about when to move them. Young fry will keep pecking at the slime on the adults, and I've seen cases where they damaged the skin of the adults to the point where infection set in.

TIME TO MOVE THE FRY

When the fry are old enough to feed without the parents, you are faced with an entirely different set of problems. You will find this to be the most demanding of all the chores required when keeping discus. Everything you have learned about discus care will be needed, and the method I am about to explain will put you to the utmost test at first. While I consider keeping young adult and fully adult discus somewhat easy, the development of their fry is not. Even in their native waters, the loss of young fry must be very high indeed. When you add all the unnatural conditions of tank rearing, you really have your work cut out for you.

FILTERS
IN THE FRY TANK

You must keep the water in the fry tank clean and have a well-working biological filter. Even with proper water changes, the filter will play a big roll in success or failure. I only use large sponge filters in the fry grow-out tanks. I try to have these filters working off a small, power head pump. The fry are very small when moved off the adults, and I have never found another filter that relieves the worry of sucking fry into the filter like the sponge rubber type. This and the large surface area of the sponge help develop a good bacterial action.

After the filter come the water conditions that must be met. I generally use the discharge water from the spawning tank to fill a ten-gallon tank where I intend to place the fry once they are relocated. You should make sure the water and filter are in good working order before moving the fry. I make the setup about five days before the expected move. It's a good idea to run the sponge filter in the spawning tank for a few days, then set it up in the new fry tank before you move the fry.

Once I actually move the fry, I adjust the water temperature to about 89°. This is done slowly. The increase in heat causes the fry to eat better and grow faster. It also discourages some disease bacteria and parasites from getting a start in the fry tank.

At this point I add two drops of malachite green to the gallon of water. I replace it when I make water changes. This helps keep parasites, such as ich and other pests, from attacking the fry. I retain this in the water until the fry are about 1 1/2 inches in size and are moved to larger quarters.

I also add a 1/4 cup of rock salt to the ten gallons of water slowly over a couple of days. This aides in keeping the newly hatched brine shrimp alive and moving in the fry tank for a longer period of time than would occur otherwise. The salt has no effect on the discus fry.

Now you must start your feeding program for the fry. Feed them newly hatched brine shrimp in small amounts, five times per day. Do not overfeed, and remove any dead shrimp that are on the bottom of the tank twice each day. Be sure to wipe down the inside glass of the tank before you make water changes. Do not allow a slime coat to build on the glass.

photo by Bing Seto

Brilliant blue discus; always looking for food

As soon as the fry can feed on fine, dry foods and finely chopped beefheart or earthworms, stop feeding them brine shrimp. You will soon notice that not all the fry are growing at the same rate. This becomes very noticeable if your feeding program is out of whack. If you are feeding them properly, only a few fish will be smaller in size than their brothers and sisters. If you are not feeding them right, you will see fry of all sizes growing at different rates.

You will of course lose some fry to natural death. But if you're doing things right, this will always be a very small percentage of the total hatch. If you do find runts in the batch, move them into a different tank and feed them extra. Sometimes this will bring them up to standard quickly. If not, cull them out and take the loss. After the fish reach a size of 1 1/2 to 2 inches, don't crowd them. Divide the batch and give them a lot of growing room in larger tanks.

If you keep the larger and smaller fish together, the big guys will bully the little fish away from the food; they will remain stunted and will eventually have to be culled.

CULLING THE FRY

While it is very hard to work for so long and spend your hard-earned money to keep and spawn your discus, it is still very important that you face culling with a plan in mind and a strong willingness to follow it through. No one wants substandard discus. That is a fact of life in the discus business.

You certainly do not want to become known as someone who produces substandard fish. So what standards should you set? My only suggestion is this: discus are supposed to be round, not oblong, with no lumps or bumps on their heads, and they should have full, beautiful fins. The color should be as bright as possible.

If at all possible, the eyes should be red. The body markings should be pleasing to view. If you are truly a discus fancier, you will know a high quality fish when you see it. I try to set my standards one grade above the best fish I have seen in the marketplace and at aquarium shows.

You can start culling at four weeks of age. Remove any fish that shows signs of poor development. As the fish grow, you can spot poorly shaped fish or fish with bad fins. I recommend that you cull lightly at four weeks, and cull again at eight weeks. Then make your final inspection at three months, or just before shipping out on a sale.

I keep only the finest of the finest for future breeders. Line breeding should stop after no more than five generations. I out cross at four generations. If you line breed too long, your fish strain becomes smaller and the fish become weaker in overall appearance and health.

Out breeding should be considered as another form of culling. You should be breeding more than one strain of discus with different bloodlines at all times. This way you can cross breed at will in order to reduce the effects of line breeding.

I must repeat: Do not give away or sell defective fish. Cull and kill those fish that do not meet your high standards. A defective discus should be considered in the same light as a diseased discus. Rid the world of it!

RECORD KEEPING:
A MUST ITEM

Few people I know like record keeping. Even with the aid of a computer and a program designed for fish breeders, it's a boring chore. In my case, it is greeted each day with a few words I would not repeat in mixed company. But it is vital that you keep good, readable records of your discus breeding activity.

The best philosophy for record keeping is, "How can you know where you're going if you don't know where you have been?" I number all the tanks in the operation. Then I assign a personal number to each fish in the breeding program. Males get even numbers, females odd numbers.

I keep a log book of the day's events in the hatchery. I make notations as I feed, change water, clean tanks, anything beyond just standard stuff. If I move a numbered fish, I make a note of it. I note the condition of pairs everyday. Notes are made about spawns that take place. Dates are marked both on the tanks and in the notebook when spawning occurs. Dates of actual hatch, the number of fry per spawn; the percentage of loss out of each spawn at two weeks, eight weeks, and after three months; all this information is placed in my computer data base.

How can you know where you're going if you don't know where you've been?

The above data collection sounds like a lot of work and a real pain in the behind, right? You're right, it is! But once you have the system worked out, it takes very little actual time to keep this information correct. The more information you have, the better later on.

I recommend that you also keep records of where your breeders came from, who the principle developer was, the date you obtained the fish, and their age, if known. Of course you will need to keep records of your sales and expenses for tax purposes. Record keeping can be fun or it can be a chore, depending upon your viewpoint.

If you do not have a computer, it might pay for you to invest in one as soon as possible, not only for record keeping, but for the wealth of information

It is vital that you keep good, readable records of your discus breeding activity. Record keeping can be fun, or it can be a chore, depending upon your viewpoint

on the internet that can be used and applied to your hatchery operation. You can buy, sell and trade through the internet. There are loads of discus people just waiting to hear from you or pass on their experiences and information.

Please consider this fact: next to a producing pair of discus, the computer is the most useful item in your business. It also just happens to be an item that can be a good tax deduction. In a way, you are letting the government underwrite part of your expense.

photo by Bing Seto

Dick Schlingmann of Germany

CHAPTER NINE

ARTIFICIALLY HATCHING
AND FEEDING NEW FRY

ONE METHOD

If you think I stressed keeping the water clean and soft up to now, you have not seen anything yet! I have been shown a half-dozen different ways to proceed with the process of artificially hatching and rearing young discus fry. I have at one time or another tried them all, none with any great degree of success. I personally prefer nature's way, let the adults do it! But the best way was explained and demonstrated to me by Mr. Bing Seto of Alameda, California. Bing is a real expert when it comes to just about all aspects of discus keeping. He collects the eggs as soon as the spawning is completed by the pair and places them in small one-gallon tanks with just an air stone and one or two drops of anti-fungus solution. When the eggs hatch and become free swimmers, he uses

a cooking baster to move the young fry to one quart, ceramic bowls. Along the top rim of the bowl he has a pre-fixed mixture of egg yolk powder. He mixes this in advance and, using water, makes a thick paste. He smears a thin coating of this in a film along the top down into the bowl about a half inch. This mixture is so thin you can hardly see it when you look at the bowl. He then fills the bowl to just the bottom edge of the film with fresh but aged clean water and then adds the young fry to the bowl.

The fry are then allowed to stay in this bowl, feeding for about four to five hours before they are transferred to a new bowl setup the same way with fresh, aged water and new food mixed as before. In the bowl, Bing uses air tubing to allow a very light, slow bubbling of air to keep the water moving slightly and provide oxygen to the water. The amount of air is adjusted so that just a few, light bubbles flow in and to the top of the water. Too much air and you wash the

photo by Bing Seto

Tending the fry.

food off the rim to the bottom and weaken the fry by making them swim in too much current. This process is repeated every four to five hours until about 11:00 p.m., at which time the fry are moved to clean bowls with no food and the lights are turned off or kept very dim until morning. At 6:00 a.m. the next morning, the process is repeated as before. He uses this system for four or five days and starts adding newly hatched brine shrimp on about the 4th day. The amount of brine shrimp is increased as the fry grow larger. When the fry are large enough to feed on pure brine shrimp, he moves them to two-gallon tanks for an additional two weeks. After two weeks in the two-gallon tanks they are transferred to 10-gallon tanks. After an additional two weeks, they are transferred to 20-gallon tanks.

Sounds simple, right? Just wait until you've tried it before jumping up and down with joy over such a simple system that could produce thousands of young fry for you! Like I said, I have tried this method and lots of others. I have seen people who are skilled in most aspects of discus keeping get so mad at failure they could cry. Seems only a few are really good at this sort of thing and a few more are able to learn it with a lot of effort. Some just never can seem to get it right!

As for me? I just have too many other things going on to waste my time at this chore. Sometimes I use one or more methods, but most of the time I just rely on mother nature to allow the adult discus to do the work of caring for their young.

I will offer this bit of advice. If you plan to artificially hatch and feed discus fry, prepare a well lighted, super clean work area for the chore. Have lots of clean, slightly aged water at hand. A working sink with hot and cold water is very helpful. You will need a washable, flat work table to hold your feeding bowls and small tanks. Good lighting that can be adjusted is also nice to have.

If you practice this hatching and feeding method, you will soon learn that a certain amount of culling starts even with these young hatchlings. Not all are born with the proper shape and form. You will also find a certain percentage just die shortly after free swimming.

Now, about the subject of proper food for newly hatched discus fry. Some will tell you that egg yolk powder is the only first food that will work. This is not true. I have seen Mr. Dick Au hatch out discus fry and start feeding them newly hatched brine shrimp as their first food and it worked!

Mr. Jack Wattley uses his own mixture of freshly boiled egg yolk mixed with both fresh, uncooked egg yolk and newly hatched brine shrimp. Who can say this does not work for Jack? He produces about 50% of his discus artificially using this formula.

Recently I printed off the internet a system used by Jeff Bodin, which he refers to as "Nineteen Simple Steps to Artificially Rearing Discus Fry." I would like to share it with you.

Nineteen Simple Steps
To artificially Rearing Discus Fry

I repeat it here in full, and credit is gratefully extended to Jeff for its use in this book. Many people react "snobbishly" to breeders who raise fry artificially, stating that eventually they (the fish) will raise their own (and they will). But I look at it this way: only a fool allows $1000.00 worth of eggs to get eaten by the parents! We can, and do, just as good a job of killing the babies ourselves!

There are two keys to raising the fry artificially: cleanliness is one; changing the water with water that is the same temperature is the other.

STEP 1   Give the parents a 1.5 -2 inch pvc pipe, 14-16 inches long to let them spawn on. pH must be below 7, and water used throughout the process must be soft (around 100ppm and US around 120-180). This helps the eggs in sticking.

STEP 2   Make sure that the males are fertilizing the eggs, otherwise any attempt is futile.

STEP 3   Wait two hours after the spawning is finished.

STEP 4   Using a one-gallon glass jar, fill it with the tank water that the parents (& eggs) are in. Put in the pvc in the jar (quickly and calmly.)

STEP 5   Place the jar in a small, five-gallon tank filled with water at 84° F (heater required?). Also put a hydrosponge (by far my personal choice in sponge filters) in the tank and turn it on. This will keep the jar warm and allow the tank to cycle.

STEP 6   Add an airstone to the jar. Turn it on medium so that there is a good current in the jar. (Don't blast the eggs, though.)

STEP 7   Add three drops of methyl blue. Other people may recommend more, but I believe that it may cause fry loss. Three drops work well and allow you to observe the eggs.

STEP 8   Wait. They will begin hatching in two days (if they are fertile and the correct water parameters/hardness/uS are present.)

STEP 9   Wait. They will start free swimming in two-three days (mostly three). They will be clogged in a bunch on the bottom of the tub during this period and will untangle when good and ready.

STEP 10   When they become free swimming, give them their first feeding. Use artificial plankton and rotifers (a.p.r.) used for feeding marine filter feeders. Add an amount the size of a small B.B.

STEP 11 Four hours later, remove the jar from the five-gallon tank and float a small rubbermaid tub in the five-gallon tank. Place the air stone in the tub (turn it off first.) Use a baster to move the fry to the little tub. Fill the tub 75% jar water and 25% tank water or until the tub is almost full. Turn on the air stone to just blip...blip...blip enough to keep the surface of the water in the tub broken. Keep the tank and tub covered to avoid cooling/evaporation/drafting on the tub.

STEP 12 Add another small amount of food as before.

STEP 13 Four hours later, do a 50% water change of the tub water using the baster. I go from the baster to another small tub before I dump the water in case I suck up some fry. If I do suck up a few, I put them back in the first tub. Replace the tub water removed with the tank water (same temperature as that in the tub to start with.) Again feed small amount of a.p.r.

photo by Bing Seto

Left to Right: Bing Seto, Manfred Gobel and Jack Wattley

STEP 14 Every 4-6 hrs do a 90% water change using the above method.
Note: eventually the 5-gallon starts to get low. Never, repeat never, fill the 5-gallon prior to filling the tub. The temperature may not be exactly the same, and if you fill the tub with colder water, the fry will go into shock and die.

STEP 15 Repeat 90% water change and feed every 4-6 hours (8 at the most.)

STEP 16 On second day of free swimming, add a tiny, *very tiny*, amount of newly hatched brine shrimp (baby brine shrimp, or b.b.s.) with every feeding. Keep using the a.p.r at this point. Keep performing step 15. The a.p.r. shows gray bellies, b.b.s. shows pink bellies in fry.

STEP 17 Continue feeding the a.p.r. and b.b.s. for one week. All bellies should show pink by the end of one week.

STEP 18   Once all the fry show pink bellies discontinue the a.p.r and continue the baby brine shrimp. Keep repeating step 15.

STEP 19   At the end of one week you will have lots of fry size discus. Turn them loose in the five-gallon tank and keep feeding them baby brine shrimp, and make regular water changes. Make sure water temperature is the same when changing water.

While I have never used this exact method, I am sure that Jeff's system will work quite well. Give it a try, and when you have tons of baby discus, think of Jeff Bodin. Thank you, Jeff, for a good system of artificially producing discus fry.

BRINE SHRIMP DOS AND DON'TS

When you get the fry to the stage where they are eating solid dry foods, your chances of being able to keep them healthy improve greatly. Feeding them brine shrimp offers about the only chance you have of getting them to that stage. But you should be aware that brine shrimp are also very bad about fouling the water and filters. The bacteria thrive on dead brine shrimp as much as the discus thrive on it as a first food. So great care must be used during the first three weeks as you develop the youngsters to the larger stages. Above all, don't overfeed!

Be sure to wipe down the insides of the fry tanks, removing the dead, uneaten shrimp and slime. Change water often.

Discus fry are without much protection from disease. Ammonia and nitrate levels increase quickly in fouled water. Proper, over-sized filters will help, but nothing replaces common sense and water changes. Make sure the water you are using has no harmful chemicals, such as chlorine. The water should be aged slightly and the temperature must be the same. Young discus are easy to shock and stress. They die quickly in unfavorable conditions. They do not have the ability to recover from their keeper's stupidity.

One problem you will notice with the use of brine shrimp is that microscopic organisms multiply very quickly. A sure sign of fouled tank conditions is the appearance of very small white worms that cover the bottom of the tank and get on the walls of the tank. If you see these critters you are not keeping your tanks clean enough. While these worms are harmless themselves, it is a warning that things are not right.

Sometimes, if uneaten brine shrimp remain in the tank, other parasites develop which attack the gills of the fry at a very young age. If you see the

...Brine shrimp are very bad about fouling the water. Discus fry are without much protection from disease...and...are easy to shock and stress. They die quickly in unfavorable conditions.

fry hanging near the top of the tank, drastic steps need to be taken to prevent fry loss. Generally, by the time you notice this effect, it is too late to save the fry.

One way I prevent this type of brine shrimp problem is by using one drop of a 37% formaldehyde and malachite green mixture per gallon of water in the grow-out tanks until the fry reach an age of four weeks. This mixture is replaced as needed with water changes. One of the "dos" about brine shrimp is to time your hatching rate. If you have young fish in need of this food, you should keep a small batch hatching out at the proper time for feeding. Don't overdo it. Brine shrimp eggs are expensive and once hatched, they do not live long. So learn to control the amounts you will need as you do your cleaning chores.

The best advice I can offer about brine shrimp is use it wisely; discontinue its use as quickly as possible.

GROWTH RATES AMONG FRY

As the young fish develop, some will grow faster than others in a given spawn. This is normal to some extent. Most likely, the larger fish will turn out to be males. This is not always the case but it is a safe bet in most batches. The ratio of males to females is impossible to predict. Generally, there are fewer males produced than females.

If your feeding program is right, most fish will develop at about the same rate. Should you see that the rate is not more or less uniform, then change your feeding program in the next batch. Smaller fish need to be separated and fed extra to bring them up to par.

CHAPTER TEN

MARKETING YOUR DISCUS

*N*ow you must think ahead a bit. As soon as you have your system in operation, you should start giving some thought to a marketing plan. Most breeders assume that if they are able to produce discus fish, somehow out of nowhere they will be able to sell their product at a nice profit. If only that were so, I would be very rich. Also, beggars would ride instead of walk!

Let's get real about the retail market for discus. If you count on the local pet store to handle your discus, you are in for a real education. It has been my experience over the last forty years or so that most retail pet stores or aquarium shops know about as much about discus as I do mining pure cheese from the deep pits of the moon. Many will talk big and make outlandish offers when you first encounter them. But it is rare that you will find a shop that will keep its word about buying your fish even if they are the best in the world. The shops that do try to handle discus for the most part wind up with runted, disease riddled, Asian fish that they buy based strictly on price. No, Mr. Retailer is not a good market! So how about the wholesaler who in turn supplies Mr. Retailer? Another lost cause? Yes for the most part. These operations are mostly always broke or near broke or getting ready to go broke. They buy strictly based upon price and shipping cost, which again translates into junk Asian discus, if they handle any at all.

Now, I don't mean to paint everyone in the business with a broad brush. There are some who do a good job with discus. But they are so rare that it would be pure chance if you were able to hook up with one and market your top quality discus fish.

You will have to look elsewhere for your market. But where? How? When? The answer is simpler than it might appear. You do sell to the retail market. You become the retailer. I prefer to refer to it as "Self Product Promotion." (S.P.P.) You develop your own customers through self-promotion. This is done by starting small and building your image as you go along.

This is done at trade shows, in articles written for local clubs and aquarium societies, and through written articles sent to national and international hobby magazines. Time spent helping others in the discus hobby alway pays great rewards sooner or later.

Accept as many speaking engagements as possible before hobby groups. Learn all you can about other discus keepers near and far. Develop your contacts via fax, telephone and E-mail.

...Sell to the retail market. Become the retailer yourself. Develop your own customers through self-promotion. This is done by starting small and building your image as you go along.

Advertising in the hobby magazines is also a good way to develop your market. There are thousands and thousands of dollars in business out there awaiting your production.

The reason? Because the pet stores and aquarium shops are missing it! And they don't really seem to care about this aspect of the business.

photo by J.E. Quarles

Dick Au packaging fish for shipment

CHAPTER ELEVEN

DISEASE

AND PHYSIOLOGY OF THE DISCUS

If you're going to invest your time and funds developing your discus business, then me should deal with the least pleasant aspect of the operation: disease and physiology of discus. I can hear the groaning out there now as I write this. But it must be covered. I am far from an expert on discus or fish diseases! But I have had over forty-five years to learn first hand what to expect.

If you are going to understand even the basics of fish disease, you must have at least a general understanding of the biological processes of a fish. Like humans and all vertebrates, they depend upon certain systems within their bodies to carry on the working functions that allow life to continue. Only a very short statement will be made about the systems most commonly affected by diseases. If you desire more information, there are lots of books that delve into this subject in much greater detail. I highly recommend that you obtain some of these books and learn as much as possible about the physiology of fish.

One book I personally consider a must for any discus keeper is entitled *Discus Health*, written by Dieter Untergasser and published by T.F.H. Publications Inc. Along with this, you should read the book *Aquariology Master Volume*, written by Dr. John B. Gratzek and published by Tetra Press.

THE INTERGUMENT OR SKIN

The skin is often the first line of defense against most diseases that affect fish. It consists of the epidermis and the dermis. The epidermis is a thin covering of five to seven cell layers and mucous glands, which are unicelluler. It contains a network of very fine capillaries. Both male and female discus produce a whitish secretion, which is the first food of the newly hatched fry. The fry, in most cases, feed upon this secretion for about two to four days before they are able to accept larger foods. Even newly hatched brine shrimp are far too large for them until this stage has been reached.

The epidermis, once broken or invaded, is often the site of infections. It is of prime importance that you observe any changes or disruptions in the skin of the fish. Treatment of skin disease is rather simple and straight forward if the problem is noticed early.

The dermis contains melanophore and is rich with blood vessels and nerves. Scales develop in the dermis and are retained in pockets very close to the surface. When a fish loses a scale, part of the epidermis is lost with it. With the formation of a new scale, the wound heals; new layers of epidermis replace what was lost or damaged. In cases of bad wounds, some scarring may show. In most cases, however, no scarring is noticable.

The scale is formed much like layers of plywood: the bony or hyadlodentine surface which is rough in texture, and the basal plate of a woven lamellar structure.

The loss of the slime layer or epidermis is a serious matter and steps must be taken to promote healing. In the event of scale loss or open wounds, never use formaldehyde. Should you do so, the formaldehyde will directly enter the blood stream through the open wound and can kill the fish very quickly.

If you are going to understand even the basics of fish disease, you must have at least a general understanding of the biological processes of the fish.

THE SKELETAL SYSTEM

We need not concern ourselves with this very much, other than to note deformed skeletal structures and cull them from the other discus as quickly as possible.

THE DIGESTIVE SYSTEMS

The size of the mouth and the arrangement of the the teeth limits the selection of foods. It would be nice if the discus had the ability to eat larger foods than is actually the case. One good factor is that cichlids have teeth to nibble and tear at their foods. It is much better to feed them small amounts more often than to give them large amounts at any one time. Discus have rather short digestive tracts or guts. They cannot eat a lot at one time, but will pick at food and hunt for food more than they actually eat. Since it is the total time the food spends in the gut that is of value to the fish, you can see that with a very short gut, feeding them small amounts four or five times per day would be of more value than just dumping in large amounts once each day. If you do that, most of the food will go foul before the discus can eat it.

Discus tend to feed at mid-water, or more often are slow, picky feeders that feed off the bottom. It is important that the bottom be free of fouled foods and waste.

All fish are infected with digestive-type worms. Most are harmless, but some are parasitic and not so harmless. This will prove to be your biggest area of concern in retaining healthy discus over long periods of time.

I have found that problems arise in this area when any aged discus are fed live blackworms and tubifex worms. It is my strong recommendation that this food be avoided. *Never feed live or dehydrated blackworms or tubifex worms to discus.*

THE RESPIRATORY SYSTEM

Water carries oxygen through the gills on currents entering through the mouth and over the gill plates. While little is ever said about it, there is some oxygen exchange through the skin of most fishes. The respiratory system in discus represents the second site of major concern in keeping discus healthy. They seem to be prone to gill parasites and diseases to a far greater extent than a lot of other fish species. Generally, when a discus becomes sick, the respiratory system is involved, or becomes involved in short order, if the problem is of any serious nature. In other words, if a discus becomes weak or stressed, watch closely for gill problems to develop if not quickly treated or the cause of the stress not promptly resolved. I strongly recommend further reading and study on the respiratory systems of fishes. To go into greater detail is beyond the scope of this book.

High oxygen content is always desirable.

THE CIRCULATORY SYSTEM

We need only concern ourselves with the function of the circulatory system in supplying blood to the gills, liver, spleen and kidney. The blood cells are the erythrocytes. They are nucleated and somewhat oval in shape. Hemoglobin is the agent that performs most of the oxygen carrying properties of the blood. Fishes have a single path of blood transfer through the heart. Deep veins transfer the blood from the organs, fins, and body tissue to the four chambers of the heart. The aeration is the function of the gills and this of course requires mechanical activity, whereby streams of water pass over the gill surfaces and out through the opercular passages. The rate of movement of the gills can be a fairly good indicator of the health of the gill area and the stress level of the discus. Rapid gill movements may signal stress or bad water conditions and possible parasite infestations. Gill movement should be smooth and regular. Also, the coloration of the gills is a good indication of proper respiratory and circulatory function.

The gills should be bright red and both sides should move in regular motion. If only one side of the gill plate is in action, or the coloration of the gills themselves is a weak pink, this indicates a problem that demands instant evaluation.

Respiratory movement can prove to be a very valuable method of determining any stressful conditions affecting your discus.

THE GAS BLADDER, EYES, AND BODY SHAPE OF DISCUS

The gas bladder, also referred to as the air bladder or swim bladder, is made up of one or more chambers. Discus, from time to time, develop into what is commonly called headstanders. In about 75% of the cases I've ever encountered, the fish terminated. Little can be done to correct this problem. A few fish may suffer this affliction and the effects can be temporary, lasting perhaps a few days or a week. If the condition continues beyond that, the condition is generally fatal. Little has been written about the cause of this condition. I have noticed that drastic food changes will cause the onset of this condition. I have never had a successful recovery unless it occurred within 48 hours.

Should your fish develop into a headstander, I would isolate it for a few days, try changing the temperature up or down a few degrees, and add a little rock salt to the food and water. If no cure occurs, it would be a kindness to simply dispose of the fish to relieve its possible suffering.

By studying the condition of the eyes in relationship to the overall shape of the head, you can gather strong evidence as to the health and soundness of most discus, from fry size to two inches, all the way old age. Discus have large eyes, which should show alertness and a clarity of vision. They should show uniformity, both being of equal size and matching coloration. Fish that appear to have extra-large eyes relative to body development should be avoided. This is sometimes noted as being bug eyed.

The head region should be full and well rounded. It should not be a bump. Any discus showing a bump or enlarged crown should be culled and not allowed to reproduce.

Discus should be round or almost circular. Oblong fish should be destroyed and never allowed to reproduce. Overall coloration is a matter of personal choice. Discus that show a curvature of the spine (mostly sold out of Asia as high fins) should be viewed with extreme care. In most cases, these are simply deformed fish, which only pollute the genetic pool of good discus.

In reference to the so-called (high finned Asian) spawned discus, all I can point out to you is that some people will do anything for a "buck."

Genetics of discus is beyond the scope of this book, however, the serious breeder striving to develop better and new strains should engage in this magical field of study.

CHAPTER TWELVE

THE PROPER PHYSICAL HANDLING OF DISCUS

Discus, from fry to adults, are delicate fish. Improper handling can cause extreme physical damage and can result in a deadly stress to the fish. Where you might be able to just dip a net into another cichlid's tank and yank it out into another tank, this is just not allowed with the discus fishes. A soft net is required when handling discus of any age or size. A calm, slow netting is best. Should the fish become frightened and dash about the tank, stop and wait a little while before proceeding with the operation. Always use what you consider to be an oversized net when handling discus.

As stated before, discus are very easy to shock or stress when subjected to movement and or water changes. When you receive fish via shipment of any type, it is best to go very slowly when making the adjustments needed to install them in a new tank or different water.

The recommended way of transfering discus is to float the bags they arrive in in the new arrangement and from time to time add a little of the new water to the bags. Of course, after a while the bags could become overfilled with water. Whatever you do, you should never add any shipping water to your tanks along with the fish. That is a big no-no.

The best way I have ever found is to have a three- to five-gallon plastic bucket or tank ready and to empty the fish along with their shipping water into this container. Then I use a length of air tubing to start a siphon from the intended new tank into the bucket containing the new arrivals. I adjust the flow of water by kinking the air tube. I can adjust from just a few drops per minute to full flow, as desired.

Generally I will allow about 1 to 2 hours for the adjustment to become complete. After that time span, I simply net the fish into their new home. This method greatly reduces the stress factor, plus you need not float the bags in the tanks.

Discus are not bad about being "jumpers." But from time to time they will become frightened and jump out of any uncovered tank. I have even had discus jump from one tank into another and out of that one into a third tank. But pure luck was with that discus that night. Most of the time when they do jump, you will find them on the fish room floor.

photos by Bing Seto

Top: Pigeon blood discus
Middle: Red pearl turquoise
Bottom: Brilliant blue discus ready to pair off.

The only thing that should be in a discus tank is the filter and an air stone, and of course the spawning cone or bricks. When netting fish, even these should be removed. Don't leave anything in the tank upon which a frightened fish can injure itself.

Of course to prevent this, all that is needed is to tightly cover the top of the tank. Because of the number of tanks in my hatchery, this is not practical. It would simply be too time consuming to work with covered tanks. But to each his own method. I do lose a fish now and again and so will you if you fail to cover the tank tops.

Just one other comment seems in order here. The only thing that should be in a discus tank is the filter and an air stone, and of course the spawning cone or bricks. When netting fish, even these should be removed. Don't leave anything in the tank upon which a frightened fish can injure itself.

In the event that an injury does occur, be aware that fungus is likely to attack any damaged area on the fish. Also, fin and tail rot is common when moving fish from aged water to fresher water. In many cases, some fin loss at the extreme ends of the fins will occur when fish are moved. This is not the same as the onset of fin rot. But be aware of the possible event and don't let fungus or fin rot get a start when moving fish. Fungus is easy to stop if caught at the start. Once it reaches the actual body of the discus, it is generally a lost cause and the fish must be terminated. I have stated before in this text, do not move fish around any more than is absolutely necessary. Spawning pairs should never be moved if you can avoid it!

CHAPTER THIRTEEN

MEDICATIONS

And Disease Treatment

> The medications listed here
> can sometimes cure a problem with your discus.
>
> → They can also kill ←
> both fish and a human child.

This last chapter offers a few suggestions about discus medications and their possible use. All the products listed here are to be considered poisonous and should be treated as poisonous substances. Extreme care should be taken to make sure all medications are in a child-safe place at all times. I suggest a locked and strictly controlled area.

The medications listed here are those that I have found to be useful in the hatchery when properly used for the right reasons. The dosages suggested are those that I have used successfully in the past. However, I must state that, if used, the reader bears full responsibility for the results. Since I cannot see or verify the symptoms, I cannot recommend specific treatments, just a general set of guidelines. It may be noted by the reader that certain brand names or products commonly sold at pet stores or aquarium shops are not listed. There is a good reason for this. I have found that most of these products are of little value in disease treatment. They are generally expensive and in most cases, in order to meet federal and state requirements are watered down to the point of being of only questionable usefulness.

It is always best to use good, pure products when treating a problem.

Acrifavin Neutral Powder 100%
> Use: The treatment of bacterial infections such as mouth fungus, saltwater ich, fin and tail rot. Also some skin parasites, oodinium (velvet), sliminess of the skin and flukes.
>
> Dosage: One drop per gallon. Treat one time only without partial water change.

Copper Sulfate Pentrahydrate
> Use: Algicide, bacterial problems, fungicide on such problems as ich, oodinium, slimy skin and flukes.
>
> Dosage: Use a liquid that is formulated so that when one drop per gallon is added to water it will equal 0.15 ppm. Never use copper with a water hardness of less than 50 ppm total water hardness.

Di-Ni-Butyl Tin Oxide Powder

Use: Kills all helmithths, acanthroceplala, digenetic tematodes, cestoda mulluscucide (snails and worms), internal and external. **Warning: Toxic to fry.**

Dosage: 4.5 grams of powder mixed and diluted with 100 ml of water. Use 1 ml of this solution per pound of food. This should equal about 1 ppm by weight.

Doxycycline Hyclate Capsules, 50mg

Use: This is a broad spectrum antibiotic derived from oxytetracycline. It works on most bacterial infections. It does not become inactive with calcium, iron or other heavy metal triplex ions as do other tetracycline antibiotics. I have found that one treatment is all that is usually needed.

Dosage: 50 mg per every 10 gallons of water.

Erythromycin Phosphate Powder

Use: Fin and tail rot, corynebacteium (kidney disease), pop eye, and most gram positive and some gram negative bacteria and fungus. Also used for black mollie disease.

Dosage: 1/4 teaspoon to 20 gallons of water.

Formaldehyde 37% Consentrate

Use: External fungicide, external protozoacide, and ectoparsites, mongenia, hirudinea, and crustacea. Can be used as a dip or for longer baths according to parts per million applied.

Dosage: One or two drops per gallon with partial water changes to be repeated for three days. If the fish appear unduly stressed, make quick water change, this reduces dosage. Formaldehyde is a strong oxidant. It reduces all organic products to other compounds. Use great care when applying. It can damage the gills and eyes of fish.

Furazolidone Powder 100%

Use: Effective against marine ulcer disease, cold water disease and protozoans. Also used in treating furunculosis in Koi fish. Mixed in food or added to water.

Dosage: 1/4 teaspoon to 15 gallons of water. This is a good starting point for unknown problems. This product will not affect later reproduction. I use it when transporting fish through air freight shipments, and when I put new fish into the hatchery.

Note: I have found this medication helpful in conditioning new tanks for use. I treat the water for two days, then make a 50% water change before adding new fish to the tank.

Kanamycin

Use: Gram negative bacteria and resistant strains of tuberculosis in fish.

Dosage: 1/4 teaspoon to 20 gallons of water.

Malachite Green (zinc free) Power 100% Pure

Use: Ich, fungus, oodinium, mouth fungus and some prevention of fungus on eggs.

Dosage: 28.4 grams to one gallon of water, then use 1 drop per gallon in treatment.

Note: I personally have found this to be one of the most useful medications in the fish room. I use it in weak solution to protect very young fry while feeding them brine shrimp. It will turn the water slightly green but this is later removed with proper water changes.

Methylene Blue (zinc free) 100% Powder

Use: Prevents egg fungus and kills some bacteria, effective in gill disease. Transports oxygen. Will affect some protozoa, is effective in the treatment of sliminess of the skin due to poor water quality. Will sometimes cure oodinium, but is not as effective as Malachite Green for this purpose.

Dosage: 24 grams makes one pint when mixed with water. Then use one or two drops per gallon.

Metronidazole (similar to flagyl)

Use: Hole-in-the-head disease (hexaita), saltwater ich, and some cases of bloat.

Dosage: One tablet of 50 mg to 20 gallons of water. Also slight amounts mixed into beefheart is effective in treating those discus that are still eating when sick. Half tablet to 1/4 lb of beefheart.

Neomycin Sulfate Powder

Use: A good disinfectant for clearing water prior to newly arriving fish. Effective against marine ulcer disease and color water disease, along with the treatment for some protozoans. Also useful in treating fununculosis.

Dosage: 1/2 teaspoon per 30 gallons of water.

Nitrozone Cl

Use: A special combination of nitrofurazone, methylene blue and salt. Good for treating newly arrived fish that have been slightly injured in shipping. Effective against marine ulcer disease, cold water disease, protozoans and some viruses.

Dosage: 1/4 teaspoon to 20 gallons of water.

Neomycin Sulfate Powder

Use: A good disinfectant for clearing water prior to newly arriving fish. Effective against marine ulcer disease and color water disease, along with the treatment for some protozoans. Also useful in treating fununculosis.

Dosage: 1/2 teaspoon per 30 gallons of water.

Nitrozone Cl

Use: A special combination of nitrofurazone, methylene blue and salt. Good for treating newly arrived fish that have been slightly injured in shipping. Effective against marine ulcer disease, cold water disease, protozoans and some viruses.

Dosage: 1/4 teaspoon to 20 gallons of water.

Oxolinic Acid Powder, 100%

Use: Antibacterial, for gram negative bacteria, used when fish seem to die for unknown reasons.

Dosage: 1/4 teaspoon to 30 gallons of water.

Oxythtracline Hydrochloride

Use: Gram positive and gram negative bacteria, cold water disease, bacterial hemorrhagic septicemia and mouth fungus.

Dosage: 1/4 teaspoon to 20 gallons of water. This is a very wide band antibacterial agent. However, due to mis-use over the years, it's effectiveness has been greatly reduced .

Potassium Permanganate Powder

Use: External parasites, external lesions, bacteria on the skin or gills. Also fungi, protozoa, monogenec, hirudinea (leeches).

Dosage: 19 mg per gallon equals 5 ppm.

Warning: Potassium permanganate is a very strong oxygenator. When properly used it is very effective in the treatment of most external conditions affecting discus fishes. Improperly used it will quickly damage the gills, eyes and skin. I have found this product to be of great value in the hatchery if used judicially with a full knowledge of its limitations and dangers. When used to treat fin rot, some loss of the fin edges is to be expected. The damage is quickly repaired and fins grow back with no trace of damage.

DISCUS DISEASE
The New Discus Epidemic

A few year ago, when the Angelfish Disease started wiping out entire hatcheries of both angelfish and discus from coast to coast, I started using potassium permanganate powder as a last resort to try and save my discus fish. The results with regard to angelfish were indeed mixed and only somewhat effective. But based upon that experience, when a short time later when the "New Discus Epidemic" or Discus Disease started causing enormous losses, I developed my own treatment using potassium permanganate. I will explain the use of this treatment here. But first you should be aware of what to look for before subjecting your fish to this treatment.

When discus develop this disease they go down very quickly. Effective treatment must be rendered very fast if you expect to save the fish. Once the disease starts, it progresses so rapidly that within five or six days all infected fish may be dead.

Discus, Uarus and Angelfish are the fish most often found to be affected by this disease. The fish will appear unwell and their color will darken. If you look closely you will notice some swelling of the mucous producing membrane. The fish quickly become apathetic and will not seem to respond to most normal stimuli. These conditions were noted by Dieter Untergasser in his book on discus diseases. I also observed this same pattern in my fish. A whitish or grayish mucous starts to appear on the fish. The area fanned by the pectoral fins generally remains free of this white film. The mucous membrane starts to flake away from the skin. When this happens, the water will experience a huge bacterial bloom. It will turn cloudy and develop a rotten smell. This can be avoided by large water changes when first noticed.

At this point you must take effective action. Reduce the number of fish per gallon of tank space. Prepare standby tanks to hold treated fish. Once treatment is started it makes little sense to put treated fish back into contaminated tanks. Make sure the nitrate level does not increase, and place extra air stones in the tank to increase oxygen in the water.

There are two methods of treatment that have proven to be effective. I will outline one proposed by Dieter Untergasser, and then explain the method I have developed.

Mr. Untergasser states in his book *Discus Health* (T.F.H.), " The disease can be cured with medications." He also states, "In my tanks and many breeders' infected fish have all been cured with the application of niomycin sulfate and nitrofurantoin." Mr. Untergasser further states that "fish afflicted with this disease must be treated in a quarantine tank at a stocking density of no more than two adult fish per 100 liters of waters." He goes on to state that treatment is effective over a three day period, with a total cure within six days.

I am confident that this treatment will work, providing you still have three to six days before the disease overtakes the fish and they die. This is a more gentle treatment than the one I developed and use in my hatchery. But as far as I am concerned, it takes too long to be effective when treating fish on death's doorstep.

The P.D.Q. Treatment
for Discus Disease
(Pretty Damn Quick)

As soon as the disease is observed, prepare extra tanks to receive the fish after treatment. I recommend 20-gallon tanks, one or two depending upon how many fish are affected. If you can have more than you actually need, so much the better for quick results.

To prepare these holding tanks, use nothing but air stones on high air flow. Make sure the water is set for a temperature of 80° to 82° F.

In a 20-gallon tank mix 1/8th teaspoon of potassium permanganate powder. I mix this in a pint of water before adding it to the tank. When the mixture is complete, net one or two fish in a large soft net and dip the net into the treatment tank while retaining the fish in the net. Use a timer and let the fish remain in the potassium bath for no longer than three full minutes. After the three minutes are up, remove the fish to the clean tanks you prepared ahead of time.

Notice: this treatment is not recommended for discus smaller than 3 inches in length. If the fish are smaller, reduce the time in the bath by half the time stated above or 1 1/2 minutes. Try to keep the number of fish per tank as small as possible.

You will notice that the fins on the fish will have browned slightly. This is the normal result of this treatment. The white slime coating should be gone or greatly reduced once the fish are treated.

Make no mistake! This treatment is strong stuff. It works by removing the slime layer on the fish. Too short a bath will not remove the infection. Too long a bath can and will damage the gills, skin and fins. This treatment is a balancing act you must learn in order to be effective.

The above treatment can be repeated after 24 hours by mixing a new bath and following the same procedures as before, but I would recommend cutting the time to 2 full minutes if a second treatment is required. If properly done, one treatment is generally all that is required. This treatment has no lasting effect on the fish and will not interfere with later reproduction. To complete the treatment and have an effective cure, you can add the antibiotic nitrofurantoin to the treated fish for a period of 48 hours. Just follow the recommended dosage for the nitrofurantoin listed on the package. Massive water changes are highly recommended for about two weeks following treatment. I personally prefer to forego the antibiotics because there is reason to believe that antibiotics can affect reproduction later. I prefer rock salt and massive water changes. The choice is open to debate.

Discus epidemic is highly infectious. Just a few drops of water from an infected tank can spread the disease to healthy tanks. Nets and other equipment that have been in contact with an infected tank need to be disinfected before being used again.

All fun things must have an ending and I think I have reached it with this final notation to my readers. I wish you all the very best of luck with your fish keeping. I hope some of the information presented in these pages proves helpful. The final point I want to make is that prevention is worth a pound of cure! Prevention of problems should always be your goal!

I promised in the text to provide you with my personal beefheart formula. I am glad to share this with you for I know it produces well-fed and healthy discus. You will find my feeding formulas for both adult discus and fry in Appendix A.

In closing this book, I once again invite you to write me expressing your views and ideas. I welcome your comments about this book and suggestions for improving it.

Photo by Jim E. Quarles

Jim E. Quarles (L), and Ian James (R), discus friend from New Zealand

My address is:

James E. Quarles
5124 Mississippi Bar Dr.
Orangevale, California 95662

A
PERSONAL
NOTE
OF THANKS

I want to thank all those people who purchased *Discus As A Hobby* and took the time to write me expressing their satisfaction with the book. While my time, of course, has limits, I always welcome comments and questions from my readers. My E-mail address is J. Reedy1633@AOL.com

I will respond to your questions and comments as time allows, and again, thank you. Tropical fish hobbyists are the greatest people on earth.

Jim.

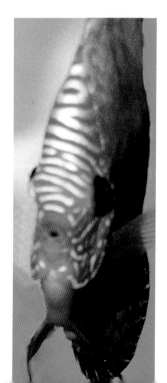

photo by Bing Seto

DISCUS AND ANGELFISH FOOD STRATEGY AND FORMULA

1. Beefheart - Recommended
2. Pigheart - Recommended
3. Flake Foods - Recommended
4. Frozen Bloodworms - Feed only occasionally
5. Any kind of insect larvae - **Not recommended** due to disease factors
6. Tubifex worms—**A VERY BIG NO-NO. I never feed these disease producers.**
7. Turkey heart - **Not recommended** - too much fat.

PREPARATION OF BEEF HEART

Clean all fat and gristle from the meat (use only pure, lean meat.) In addition, you might choose to add any or all of the following items: spinach, dry fish food, multi-vitamins, shrimp meat, raw egg yolk, wheat germ, peas, lettuce, pears, bananas, crab meat, cauliflower, plankton.

I add a selection of the above items uncooked to a high speed blender and chop to a fine grain. Then I add cooked oatmeal and raw wheat germ. I again blend and chop this to as fine a mixture as possible. I then place the finished product into ziplock sand-

FOOD STRATEGY AND FORMULA (cont)

wich bags and flatten with a rolling pin. Stack them five high and freeze them until needed.

You can cut strips off with a knife or just use your fingers to break off what you need to feed the fish. In addition to the above, I grind pure beefheart without any additions to feed to young fry. This must be chopped super fine for small fish.

FEEDING STRATEGY

1. Adult fish: beefheart mixture three times a day.
2. Adult fish: frozen bloodworms one or two times per week .
3. Young adult fish: feed five or more times per day.
They are given the same food as the adults only more often.

FRY FEEDING

1. Fourteen to thirty days: newly hatched brine shrimp five times per day. Add multi-vitamins after rinsing brine shrimp clean with fresh water.

Success With Discus
by Jim E. Quarles

Cover design: Roberta Steele
Cover photo: Bing Seto
Book design: Jill Cremer
Printing by Pacific Rim International Printing, Inc.